ADMINISTRATION, ETHICS AND DEMOCRACY

Administration, Ethics and Democracy

ØJVIND LARSEN

Ashgate

Aldershot • Burlington USA • Singapore • Sydney

Published by
Ashgate Publishing Ltd
Gower House
Croft Road
Aldershot
Hants GU11 3HR
England

Ashgate Publishing Company
131 Main Street
Burlington
Vermont 05401
USA

Ashgate website: http://www.ashgate.com

British Library Cataloguing in Publication Data
Larsen, Øjvind
Administration, ethics and democracy
1. Public administration - Moral and ethical aspects
I. Title
351'.01

Library of Congress Catalog Card Number: 00-132585

ISBN 0 7546 1221 X

Printed and bound by Athenaeum Press, Ltd.,
Gateshead, Tyne & Wear.

Contents

Introduction

Ethics is a new research area in the study of administration. Until recently, very few people looked at the relationship between ethics and administration. Administration was politically steered through democratic institutions, which functioned in such a manner so as to make the questioning of the relationship between ethics and administration unnecessary. This is no longer the case. In recent years, a number of scandals have surfaced in the administration of the state, making the relationship between administration and ethics one of the central matters both in the study and practice of administration. As an example of this I would point to the Tamil Affair, which sent shockwaves through the Danish civil service system, and has equally set its impression on Denmark's political system.

An Example

To illustrate the matter of ethics for administrators, I will initially begin with an example from the Tamil Affair, taken from an investigative hearing of the Director of the Danish Immigration Service, Frederik Schydt, as reported in the newspaper *Information*:

> As the first witness in the hearings on the Tamil Affair, Frederik Schydt, the Director for the Danish Immigration Service refused to answer a question posed by the leader of the investigation, High Court Judge Mogens Hornslet. After advice from his legal counsel, lawyer Bjørn Høberg-Petersen, Schydt would not confirm a discrepancy between the description he gave of the Tamil Affair in a private note written on 6 December, 1988 and the explanation he gave to the Danish parliament's ombudsman later in the same month.
>
> On 6 December, Frederik Schydt wrote to himself that permission for family reunification for 300 Tamil refugees was ready to be sent to the Danish Immigration Service. But on 18 December, when he was asked for a written explanation by the Parliamentary Ombudsman, Hans Gammeltoft-Hansen, as to why the Directorate for Immigration had not expedited the Tamil cases, he

> wrote, among other things, that the Directorate 'necessarily had to prioritize'. Neither the investigating committee's prosecutors, the lawyer Henrik Holm-Nielsen nor Mogens Hornslet could figure out what 'necessary prioritizing' was when 300 permits were ready to be sent out.
>
> In order to answer the question in a satisfying manner for Schydt, Højberg-Hansen found it necessary to take over the role of prosecutor in order to steer his client's answers. This led to the explanation that Schydt had answered the question about prioritizing in a general manner, and it was unquestionable that the Directorate generally had insufficient resources. Holm-Nielsen pointed out that the remark about 'necessary prioritizing' was part of a wider context, where both before and after this remark there was specific mention of the Tamil cases, but this did not make Schydt change his explanation. 'I don't think we will come any further on this matter' stated Mogens Hornslet.
>
> Additionally, Schydt did not believe that the Directorate for Immigration could have written anything other than what they did in reply to the Ombudsman. Even though Schydt, more than anyone else, knew that the lowering of the priority of the immigration of Tamil family members was not based on a lack of resources at the Directorate, but solely was a result of an order from the then Minister of Justice, Erik Ninn-Hansen, he did not feel that he could write the truth to the Ombudsman. 'It would be a gross violation of my loyalty obligation' explained Schydt.[1]

This example shows the dilemma of the civil servant with crystal clarity. Schydt was quite aware that it was unlawful to hinder the reunification of Tamil families. It is also, therefore, that he notes in his diary on 6 December that everything is in order for the 300 family reunification cases. What is of interest to us here is Schydt's notes in his diary. The diary is Schydt's final public space. In his diary he can express himself openly, as his diary is strictly his own public space. It is private. But it is still public in a sense, for as long as Schydt expresses himself in writing, he has the opportunity to subjectify his consciousness in a way which allows him to enter into dialogue with it. This consciousness can then, at a later stage, enter into another public space as evidence that he had these considerations. This has led to Schydt's diary entries on the Tamil Affair being seen as a strategic action, a type of 'life insurance', as Carsten Henrichsen called it.[2] It is possible to approach it in this way. But even if this is the case, it does not change the principal relationship, that the problem surrounding the reunification of the families of Tamil refugees caused a personal conflict for Schydt and that he believed that he could only express this personal ethical issue in the most limited public space that exists, a diary.

This comes clearly to the surface on 18 December when Schydt, on behalf of the Directorate, must reply in writing to the Parliamentary Ombudsman, Hans Gammeltoft-Hansen, as to why the Directorate has not expedited the Tamil cases. As mentioned above, the reason given was that the Directorate had to set priorities. The investigation committee's prosecutor could not reconcile this explanation in light of the diary entry from 6 December because it cannot be reconciled. What is interesting for us is *what* is irreconcilable and *why* it is irreconcilable.

The fact is that in the diary it is Schydt the *person* who expresses himself, while in the response to the Ombudsman, it is Schydt in the *role* of the Director for the Directorate for Immigration who expresses himself. Schydt himself explains this schizophrenia. As a civil servant, he is bound by obligations of loyalty to the Minister of Justice. In Schydt's own words, 'it would be a gross violation of my loyalty obligation' to write the truth to the Ombudsman.

Here, there is a split between the person and the role. In this split, Schydt elected to allow the role to go before the person. This example shows that an administrator can be bound into the bureaucratic system to such a degree that he ends up in a situation where he chooses to relinquish himself as a person. The contradiction in this choice though, is that it is the person who is held accountable for the actions which are taken under the role. This is precisely what took place in the investigation proceedings of the Tamil Affair.

There is no reason to believe that what has just been described is exceptional in the relationship between the person and the role of administrator. On the contrary, this contradiction we have seen is what Max Weber would call an ideal typical situation. The split is so clear in this case because both the person and the role are represented, each in their own independent expression, in the diary and the reply to the Ombudsman and these two statements are internally irreconcilable.

The Principle

As the example given above shows, the administrator's ethical dilemma becomes apparent the moment contradictory demands are made on him. In this situation, the administrator is brought into a conflict where he can no longer remain exclusively in his role. He is forced to personally take a position on how he will act. It is precisely in this meaning that I speak of ethics. According to my understanding, ethics is about the personal position taken on a real matter in a situation for which direct prescriptions based on ordinary social norms or customs (which is what ordinary norms used to be called) are lacking.

The acute situation from the Tamil Affair is not in its content unique. It only brings to light the principle that normally applies to administrators. In recent years, a number of other cases have occurred which have made it clear that the general problem of ethics and administration is a common and serious matter. The many cases can be interpreted as indicative of a general breakdown in the way administration is understood. The previous and current understanding is built first and foremost on the idea that it is possible to steer administration politically through democratic decisions and that these decisions will be carried out with the assistance of an administration organized on a hierarchy of command. Administration, in other words, is built upon a democratic principle of obedience. The administrator is to act in obedience to the orders he receives from his superiors. In the final instance, the administrator is responsible to democratically elected politicians. For as long as politicians are elected by democratic institutions, there is a direct connection to the citizens in civil society.

This relatively simple model no longer holds. It has been ripped apart by the advance of modern society. This advance not only affects individuals, but also social institutions.

On the one side, the advance of modern society results in increasing individualization.[3] The individual is no longer a product of his local context and the norms found in this context. To an increasing extent, individuals in modern society are referred back to themselves when they need to decide how to act. Obedience is therefore no longer an adequate form of social action. The individual wants an explanation as to why he should act in a particular manner. Ethics has therefore become a central issue in modern society. This can be seen in how important ethics has become in the public discourse. Newspapers are full of discussions about ethical issues. There is no longer any norm which is rooted in modern society. All norms are open for discussion and it is up to the individual to take a stand on them. In this way, responsibility for one's actions is laid directly on the individual. One should also be able to account for the norms one acts from. It is no longer sufficient to be responsible to a preestablished norm. It is the norms themselves that are open to debate. This increases the need to hold public discussions about norms. Ultimately, there is an increased opportunity for individuals to act responsibly in the social settings in which they find themselves.

On the other hand, however, there is another fundamental tendency in the advance of modern society which is expressed in the increasing bureaucratization of modern society. Previously, administration consisted of the state's limited intervention in civil society. This is no longer the case. In modern welfare societies, nearly all social life passes through public administration. This is either direct or indirect. It is no exaggeration to speak of an administrative society. Additionally, particular areas of public administration establish themselves as self-referential systems, which primarily see their goal as sustaining themselves in relation to other 'systems', which are seen as a foreign environment by the individual system. These administrative systems reproduce themselves as independent systems which are dominated by one-sided views of social life.

The advance of modern society is also characterized by a dynamic contradiction between, on the one hand, increasing individualization with a related normative liberalization and, on the other hand, increasing mediation of social life through bureaucratic systems. The administrator finds himself caught directly between these two contradictory tendencies. On the one hand, he, like all other members of society is personally affected by the normative liberalization of modern society. On the other hand, he must fulfill his role as an administrator within a particular administrative system. A number of conflicting demands are hereby made on the individual administrator, who is partly attached to the particular administrative system, and partly to other systems. First and foremost this revolves around demands made by law, the administrator's superiors, the administrator's profession and civil society. The administrator has to meet these demands to maintain his role. It is paradoxical that it is the person who is responsible for fulfilling these demands. A role cannot be held responsible for anything, only a person can.

The administrator as a person must take a position on how he will act in his role, but the role is determined by demands which are formulated external to the individual administrator. In this way the administrator comes to stand in the centre of the contradictions of modern society. He is continuously faced with making personal choices in relation to systemically oriented demands. In this way, the issue of ethics is of increasing relevance to the administrator.

It is not just the relevance of ethics to administrators that is an issue of continuing importance. It has implications for the wider public, as it touches upon our general understanding of administration in modern democratic welfare societies. In the modern welfare society, the administrator is not just a civil servant in a ministry or municipality. The administrator is also the person who takes care of and plays a direct part in the citizen's life through the institutions of civil society. Home-assistance nurses, kindergarten teachers, social assistance advisors and school teachers are all examples of administrators for whom the relationship between ethics and administration is a fundamental issue.[4]

My thesis is that in so far as the individual administrator, to an increasing extent, is forced to make ethical choices on which he personally must take a position, it is of absolute importance to open up public discussion about these choices. It is not just important that the individual administrator is not left alone in his ethical choices. It is also of equal importance for citizens and the political community in general who are also dependent on these decisions. In this way, there is an essential tie that binds administration, ethics and democracy together in modern society.

Analysis and Structure

The intention of this book is to examine the ethical issues confronting administrators. Two demands should be put to such an undertaking. One is that the analysis of ethical problems should be done in a way which shows a comprehensive understanding of administration. The other is that the treatment of ethics should take reference to the wider discussions of ethics in contemporary philosophy. In other words, such an analysis should comprise both sociological and philosophical approaches to the matter of administrative ethics. The first thing that needs to be done is to disclose *in what way* the administrator's ethical dilemma arises. This is a sociological task. The second task is to present a principal analysis of *what* the administrator's ethical dilemma consists of. This is a philosophical matter.

The point where these two perspectives meet is in the discourses which arise out of administrative institutions. The word 'discourse' derives from the French word *discourse* which means to speak or lecture. Discourse is used to categorize linguistic expressions, whether they are oral or written in character. From a sociological perspective, it is possible to disclose the administrator's ethical dilemma by looking at the various discourses within administration. These very same discourses are of interest from a philosophical perspective when matters of principle in the administrator's ethical dilemma are examined.

This book takes the following form. Chapter 1 shows that ethics in general has become more important in modern society due to the fact that norms can no longer be justified merely by referring to tradition, religion or metaphysics. This does not necessarily lead to a fundamental nihilism, as we find in Max Weber's analysis of modern society. Jürgen Habermas has shown that modernity opens up the opportunity for a communicative justification of norms in modern society. This matter is taken up in Chapter 1 in the discussion of the forms of rationality in modern society. It is within this context that the discussion of the relationship between communicative and goal-oriented rational action is of interest. According to Habermas, modern society cannot exclusively be reproduced communicatively. According to Habermas, it is necessary that communication is conveyed through systems. This mediation can, however, lead to systems taking over communication that is necessary for the reproduction of social relations in society.

This contradiction between communication and the establishment of systems is taken up in Chapter 2, with special attention to modern politics and administration. Based on the work of Claude Lefort and Habermas, I show that modern politics fundamentally is communicatively founded, but that it also has a tendency to take on a strategic, goal-oriented rational character. In the subsequent examination of modern administration, the analysis is complemented with the inclusion of theories from Weber and Luhmann, to show that goal-oriented rationality predominates in administration, while at the same time administrations have a tendency to solidify themselves as independent systems.

In summary, the first two chapters argue that a number of forms of rationality are possible in modern society. First, goal-oriented rational action tends to dominate over communicative action. Second, there is a tendency for goal-oriented rational action to be replaced by a systemic rationality in politics and administration. It is upon this background that the modern administrator is analyzed in Chapter 3.

The problem in this context is whether the modern administrator acts exclusively in accordance with systemic demands, or if there are internal limits for this form of rationality which opens the opportunity for communicative action. The point of departure here is in the different challenges to the administrator. It is shown that it is the contradictory demands made on the administrator which force him to take an individual decision on how he will act. This is where the ethical dilemmas of the administrator have come to the surface, requiring him to justify his norms for acting in the chosen manner in a situation in which the customary references for action have lost their direct relevance.

To illuminate this dilemma, in Chapter 4 I take up the administrative ethic that Weber put forward in his lecture *Politik als Beruf*. In this lecture, Weber posits that the duty of an administrator requires that he supress his own will and carry out the will of his superiors. This view of the administrator's ethical dilemma is in principle correct, but no longer holds when the administrator is subject to contradictory demands. In such a situation simple obedience is impossible. Here, we come to the point where the administrator has to make up his mind as to how he will act, and here there is a similarity between the politician's and the administrator's ethical dilemma. They both are circumscribed by goal-oriented rational action, and they both can be held accountable for how they act. At this point I introduce Karl-Otto Apel's ethics of responsibility and conclude, in agreement with Apel, that the communicative principle cannot overcome the reality principle. The principle of power is the dominant principle in both politics and administration.

Based on the preceding argument, I come to my idea of the negative or critical ethic, which consists of the possibility for formulating a *justified position* against certain demands from one of the authorities to which the administrator is responsible. In this connection Habermas speaks of '*Das Nein-sagen-können*', the 'opportunity to say no'.[5] The administrator must have the *possibility to say no*. Freedom of expression in administration then becomes a central issue, in that it is only possible for the administrator to put forward his justified positions if he is free to do so. At this point in Chapter 5, we reach the necessity of institutionalizing a form of public freedom of speech or expression. The problem is, however, that there are power relations in administration which can suppress the realization of freedom of expression. It is possible to formally institutionalize freedom of expression, but a change in the culture of administration is required to realize freedom of expression. The idea of the many, competing publics enters at this point. The existence of many, competing publics opens the possibility that different institutions will mutually expose each other. The cultural question concerning the extent to which the individual administrator is motivated to take part in such publics remains. It is in this connection that I, in Chapter 6, put forward my idea about the establishment of an ethic for the administrator. It should be possible to change the administrative culture in a way that it becomes natural for the individual administrator to express himself with regard to ethical dilemmas within the administration. This would be a change in administration in accordance with the fundamental principle of democracy. Therefore, it is important in this work to show that there is a direct connection between administration, ethics and democracy.

What remains, however, is the fact that even the best institutional improvements in administration and administrative culture cannot change the principal relation situations that administrators will continue to be put in, where they are confronted by contradictory demands over which they have to make individual choices and to bear responsibility for their actions. There are no final institutional solutions to ethical problems. However, *institutional possibilities* can be created to enable the administrator to act ethically.

As is evident, the theories of Weber and Habermas are central to this work. The centrality of Weber stems from, in my interpretation of his work, his formulation and description of the central issue in Western culture as a question of rationality, and that he thereby has shown that the matter of rationality is also of central importance when looking at administration. Habermas plays a central role through his theory of communicative action which is based on a critique of Weber and gives a more fruitful explanation of Western culture, in that he finds that there is communicative, and therefore, democratic potential in our culture which we have the opportunity to realize. In this way, Habermas's theory opens up the opportunity to reform administration in a way that improves the *institutional opportunities* for the administrator to act ethically.

As mentioned, in this work I try to unite the sociological with the philosophical perspective on the administrator's ethical dilemma. The sociological perspective can, through Weber, be termed ideal-typical. In his description of the sociological ideal type, Weber emphasizes that he is not referring to a moral ideal.[6] The sociological ideal type has nothing to do with morality. Weber states, for example, that even the brothel has its sociological ideal type. The purpose of the sociological ideal type is merely to highlight the general characteristics in a social relation or institution. I am interested in the general sociological aspects of the administrator's ethical situation. Therefore, I only introduce specific ethical conflicts to illustrate the general issue. The philosophical perspective can, in accord with Adorno, be called *critically* Kantian. In the Kantian tradition, it is not possible to put forward a general, affirmative proposal on the so-called 'good life'. It is only possible to speak generally about how we can talk about the ethical. In the *critical* Kantian tradition, ethics can only be treated *negatively.*[7] In this tradition it is only possible to speak of the *objectionable*. The reader will, therefore, search in vain if looking for how concrete ethical problems in administration are appropriately to be solved. In this work there are only considerations about *how one can think about* ethical conflicts in administration. This is, however, a decisive step because it forms the precondition for understanding and taking a position on concrete ethical conflicts in administration.

1 Modern Society

Existence and Institution

Ethical dilemmas are not something one chooses to have. Ethical dilemmas are something one suddenly is cast into and something from which one cannot escape. Ethical dilemmas are always fundamentally of an existential character. This is also true for the administrator. An ethical dilemma can suddenly arise in the course of handling routine matters, casting the administrator into a predicament he cannot avoid. As exemplified in the introduction to this book, Frederik Schydt, the Director of the Danish Immigration Service was suddenly confronted with an acute ethical dilemma when the Minister of Justice, Erik Ninn Hansen gave him an order which was unlawful. Schydt was forced to decide whether he should obey the law, or obey the orders of his superior.

The acute existential dimension of the administrator's ethical situation makes it appropriate to apply what could be called an existential phenomenological perspective to the situation. This perspective, however, is not sufficient to understand the ethical situation of the administrator. The administrator's ethical dilemma is not just something that suddenly appears in a certain situation. It is, at the same time a summary expression of the social, institutionally conveyed complexity of a particular situation. It is this latter relationship I want to analyze.

As noted in the introduction, no general advice can be given for how an individual administrator should act in a particular situation. On the other hand, it is possible to say something about the general ethical situation of the administrator in which he alone must decide how he will act. But in order to do this, it is necessary to look at how the administrator's ethical situation takes a rather particular form in modern society. With reference to Hegel's philosophy of law, one could say that every social phenomenon must be presented in its immediate form, while at the same time being presented as a *mediated institutional* relation.[8]

This is the reason why I begin by giving a general description of the principles of modern society, and then in the following chapter look at the extent to which these principles institutionally apply or impact upon politics and administration. It is only upon this institutionally mediated background that I can, in Chapter 3, begin to present the administrator's ethical situation as a direct, existential relationship into which he is cast.

Modernity in Change

That which most characterizes modern society is that it is in a permanent process of change. 'All that is solid melts into air' is the title of Marshall Berman's book in which he describes how modernity proceeds.[9] Permanent change is what distinguishes modern society. All other social formations in history have been characterized by stability. This is why they are also called traditional societies. What is meant by this is that these societies were reproduced by the repetition of set patterns in production, socialization, norm formation, etc. Every violent change was a threat to these societies' existence. What characterizes modern society is that it cannot exist as a stable society. Modern society can only exist if new conflicts are created for which attempts are made at resolution, creating new situations and conflicts. This situation, which we soon will examine more closely holds for all realms of life; politics, administration, production, the family, socialization, the formation of norms, art, etc.

Breaking with Tradition, Religion and Metaphysics

Continuous change has decisive importance for the way people orient themselves. In traditional society, one orients oneself after tradition, religion or metaphysics, depending on what society one finds oneself in. Tradition prescribed how the individual should act, and there was no great uncertainty about what was expected of the individual over the course of his life. In religion, the higher meaning of existence was formulated, and it was not possible to question its meaning. This would have lead to the individual falling out of society, which was the equivalent of being eradicated. In western culture, religion was supplemented by metaphysical considerations about the place of humans in the great God-given or natural order.

Characteristic of the modern advance is that these three reference points – religion, metaphysics and tradition lose their importance. The individual in modern society is no longer bound to a particular rooted tradition from cradle to grave. Religion can no longer provide the answer to life's definite meaning, and there is no longer a metaphysic which can take the place of religion. There are, in other words, no longer any preordained, directly valid references from which the modern individual can orient his life.

The Rational Character of Modern Society

It would be wrong here to conclude that the modern person stands totally alone with regard to orienting himself. On the contrary, the modern advance has a very definite character in western society which offers new possibilities for orientation. This was first and foremost described by Max Weber.

In the preface to the collection of his writings on the sociology of religion, Weber puts forward the universal historical idea that in the West, and only in the West, cultural phenomena that arose comprised part of a line of development of universal importance and validity.[10] To Weber, it was not yet totally clear whether there was an internal connection or just a contingent connection between the modern rupture and that which he calls western rationalism, by which he meant the unique western rationalization of religion, science, art, economics, and state bureaucracy.[11] To understand the modern rupture, one must understand the special characteristics of western rationalism and explain its origin.

Any attempt to make such an explanation must, according to Weber, take into account the economic conditions of the origin of western rationalism due to the fundamental importance of the economy.[12] This is the explanatory model we find in the work of Karl Marx.[13] But this perspective, in which forces of production lead to a change in relations of production, according to Weber, should not lead to leaving the reverse causality out of the analysis. Just as the origin of economic rationalism is dependent on rational technology and rational law, it is also, according to Weber, dependent on people's ability and disposition towards particular forms of practical, rational ways of living. Where this is intertwined with restraints of a religious nature, according to Weber, the development of an economically rational way of life meets strong internal resistance.[14]

The Importance of Protestantism

In *The Protestant Ethic and the Spirit of Capitalism*, Weber shows how Protestantism not only contributed to triumphing over the restraints on an economically rational way of life, but also how the powers of the soul were invested in it. Weber presents a very refined sociology of religious analysis, of how spiritual powers, which in the Catholic form of Middle Age Christianity were bound to religious salvation, were liberated from this connection, which from an economic rationality perspective can be seen as a constraint, and were invested in economic activity.

Calvinism is especially significant in this regard. Calvinism had a strong theological understanding of predestination, the belief that God has already decided who is saved and who is not, regardless of human action. This theological conception is turned, in the bourgeois economic interpretation, entirely around in the sense that of course Christians cannot know about God's preordained plans; but on the other hand, God in his goodness and power would not want the saved to live in misery on earth. This reasoning was turned around once again to give an understanding that when things go well for an individual, it must be *a sign* that God has selected that person for salvation.

With this perversion of the doctrine of predestination, the way is paved for the previously religiously bound energies to be applied rationally to obtain economic wealth in order to acquire the sign or trait of predestined salvation. The goal of this economically rational way of life is predetermined by God. The problem is to find adequate means to rationally reach this goal. In this way, according to Weber, goal-rational action is introduced as the fundamental form of rational action in western culture. This form of rationality is fundamental to the capitalist economic form, which aims precisely for the increased accumulation of capital. Protestantism, and especially Calvinism, from a sociology of religion perspective, becomes the driving force of the cultural revolution pushing the centre of spiritual energies out of the religious sphere and into the temporal, where spiritual characteristics are then detected in economically rational behavior.

Weber shows by extension how, as capitalism consolidates, economically rational action is wrested from its original religious constraints and becomes a goal in itself. The accumulation of wealth then becomes a goal in itself.

Weber then, in analyzing English Puritanism and Methodism, shows how economically rational action consolidates itself in the form of a bourgeois ethics of calling.[15] Weber writes that standing in God's full mercy and to be clearly blessed by Him not only enabled the bourgeois capitalist – when he kept to the formally correct parameters, had an externally apparent moral disposition and did not use his wealth for opulence – to pursue his business interests, it *obliged* him to do so.[16] According to Weber, the power of religious asceticism also brought to the capitalist sober, conscientious and eager workers who saw their work as a God given goal in their life. Furthermore, according to Weber, consciousness of God's grace gave the bourgeois capitalist the calming security that the unequal distribution of goods on Earth was part of God's plan, in that by way of these differences, as well as individually distributed salvation, God proceeded with his secret, inscrutable ends. Understanding work as a 'calling', according to Weber, also became a characteristic of the modern worker, just as the equivalent understanding of income was for the employer. Through this ethic of calling, it was possible to approach rationally both work and income or profit. In both cases it was a matter of doing God's will, which gave meaning to the goal rational activity.

It is Weber's point that the bourgeois ethic of calling liberated itself from its religious origin as capitalism consolidated. Income became a goal in itself, work became a goal in itself, neither being pursued any longer for the glory of God. At this point we arrive at what Weber calls the spirit of capitalism.[17] Weber then puts forward his description of modern society as an 'iron cage':

> The Puritan wanted to work in a calling; we are forced to do so. For when asceticism was carried out of monastic cells into everyday life, and began to dominate worldly morality, it did its part in building the tremendous cosmos of the modern economic order. This order is now bound to the technical and economic conditions of machine production which to-day determine the lives of all the individuals who are born into this mechanism, not only those directly concerned with economic acquisition, with irresistible force. Perhaps it will so determine them until the last ton of fossilized coal is burnt. In Baxter's view the care for external goods should lie on the shoulders of the 'saint like a light cloak, which can be thrown aside at any moment'. But fate decreed that the cloak should become an iron cage.
>
> Since asceticism undertook to remodel the world and to work out its ideals in the world, material goods have gained an increasing and finally an inexorable

> power over the lives of men as no previous period in history. To-day the spirit of religious asceticism – whether finally, who knows? – has escaped from the cage. But victorious capitalism, since it rests on mechanical foundations, needs its support no longer. The rosy blush of its laughing heir, the Enlightenment, seems also to be irretrievably fading, and the idea of duty in one's calling prowls about in our lives like the ghost of dead religious beliefs. Where the fulfillment of the calling cannot directly be related to the highest spiritual and cultural values, or when on the other hand, it need not be felt simply as economic compulsion, the individual generally abandons the attempt to justify it at all. In the field of its highest development, in the United States, the pursuit of wealth, stripped of its religious and ethical meaning, tends to become associated with purely mundane passions, which often actually give it the character of sport.
>
> No one knows who will live in this cage in the future, or whether at the end of this tremendous development, entirely new prophets will arise, or there will be a great rebirth of old ideas and ideals, or, if neither, mechanized petrification, embellished with a sort of convulsive self-importance. For of the last stage of this cultural development, it might well be truly said: 'Specialists without spirit, sensualists without heart; this nullity imagines that it has attained a level of civilization never before achieved.' [18]

In this diagnosis, goal-oriented rationality has completely triumphed as the social and cultural form of rationality. What is worse though, is that this triumph implies a loss of both freedom and meaning. Goal-oriented rationality becomes a compulsion, which ultimately is meaningless, because the religious dimension that previously partly gave both freedom and meaning to this form of rationality has disappeared. The calling has become a meaningless relic of the past, and activity attached to a calling is only enforced through compulsion.

Habermas's Critique of Weber's Analysis of Modernity

Weber's empirical investigation in *The Protestant Ethic and the Spirit of Capitalism* concentrated solely on the origin of capitalism and how goal-oriented rationality became institutionalized as the dominant form of rationality. This has to do with social rationalization, which means the establishment of one or more forms of rationality in a society. In Weber's investigation, social rationalization is identified only with the form of rationality which came to be dominant in modern capitalist society. At the same time, Weber offers a very pessimistic diagnosis. It is here that Habermas begins his critique which we will look at below.

The problem is that Weber identifies rationalizing with the historically specific form of rationality which has evolved in western culture. In this way Weber, according to Habermas, has not seized the opportunity to differentiate between the cultural rationalization of forms of understanding and the historical rationalization of forms of action. Such a differentiation would have given Weber the opportunity to erect a critical standard by which to evaluate actual historical rationalization, in which goal-oriented rationality became dominant.[19] According to Habermas, what is missing is a standard for evaluating the pessimistic diagnosis of contemporary society which Weber puts forward in *The Protestant Ethic and the Spirit of Capitalism*. In the following discussion, I will look at how Habermas tries to solve this problem.

Habermas introduces a differentiation between, on the one hand, a rationalization of the sphere of cultural value and, on the other hand, a rationalization of the social order of life and action systems.[20] What is understood by the sphere of cultural value is a particularly limited area of cultural values. A cultural value sphere can be rationalized. What is meant by this is that one can inquire about the validity of existing cultural values from certain set criteria, which also can be critically tested. What is understood by a social order of life or an action system is the*unification* of a rationalized sphere of cultural value with the social interests which apply in respective areas.

The sphere of cultural value is divided into three rationality complexes. A rationality complex is the limiting of a particular form of rationality which belongs to particular cultural values. The cognitive-instrumental rationality complex belongs with science, technology and social technology. The moral-practical rationality complex belongs with morality and law. The aesthetic-practical rationality complex belongs with eroticism and art.[21] The three rationality complexes belong with the three spheres of cultural value, in which modern European culture historically has become differentiated.

Based on these three spheres of cultural value, Habermas maintains that the *criterion* for *successful* cultural rationalization is that it does *not* proceed selectively.[22] By this Habermas means that the three spheres of cultural value are attached to their respective action systems in such a way that the production and conveying of knowledge is secured, and that this production through expert cultures is mediated to everyday life practices and made useful for social action systems. Finally, the spheres of cultural value are institutionalized in such a way that the corresponding life orders can be sufficiently autonomous in relation to other life orders.

A *selective* and therefore *unsuccessful* rationalization pattern means that at least one of the three spheres of cultural value has not been worked through systematically, or that it has *not* been sufficiently institutionalized as a life order, or that one life order dominates to the extent that it forces on other life orders an alien form of rationality.[23] Weber, according to Habermas, has not established such 'counterfactual' considerations about a possibly *unsuccessful* rationalization of the cultural value spheres. Habermas believes, however, that in this way the criteria for successful rationalization of the spheres of cultural value are established which can then be applied to Weber's investigation. These criteria can be used to evaluate the rationalization of western culture which Weber presents.

Based on these criteria, the relationship between the three spheres of cultural value and their respective life orders in Weber's theory look like this:[24]

Cognitive-instrumental rationality is culturally institutionalized through science. At the same time, the autonomous development of the economic and political life orders is completed, which determines the structure of bourgeois society in accordance with the standard of formal rationality.

Aesthetic-practical rationality is culturally institutionalized in art. Art, however, does not have a structure creating effect on society in general; it is not completed in a life order. It does, however, form the basis for 'the sensualist's' hedonistic life style, which seeks inner liberation from the press of theoretical and practical rationality which the 'specialist' has trumped through in everyday life, science, economics and the state.

Habermas's interpretation of Weber's theory is that cognitive-instrumental rationality has become dominant both culturally and in the life order of modern society and that aesthetic-practical rationality can only sublimate the dominance of the specialist's goal-oriented rationality through the sensualist's internal flight from reality. Modern man is essentially split into two: the specialist without spirit and a sensualist without a heart.

At the same time, according to Habermas's interpretation of Weber, moral-practical rationality is incompatible with the specialist and sensualist.

These two 'types' unify to form a life order which prohibits the communicatively mediated reconciliation between individuals. This is not just to do with the religious brotherhood ethic which, according to Habermas, to a large extent becomes 'milled' between the specialist and sensualist mill stones.[25] The Protestant calling ethic has surely formed the foundation for the beginning of modernization, but the process of modernization, according to Habermas's interpretation of Weber, erodes with retroactive power the Protestant value rational foundation for goal-oriented rational action. In this interpretation, the Protestant dispositional ethic which forms the moral foundation of the calling is washed away by a utilitarian-oriented instrumental attitude towards work. The religious need for meaning which, according to Weber's sociology of religion, was the original driving force for all forms of rationalizing culture and society and consisted of a need for 'the course of history, insofar as it touches human interests, must be a *meaningful* history' is a need which, according to Weber, remains unfulfilled.[26]

According to Weber, what is paradoxical about social rationalization is that the highest value in the culture, the perfection of the cultural person, ends up in meaninglessness.[27] Weber cannot resolve this contradiction. According to Habermas, this is because of two things.[28] The first is that Weber does not realize that what is going on is a *selective* rationalization of the sphere of cultural value and their respective life orders, and that as a consequence, this is *a particular form* of differentiation. To Weber, it is *differentiation in itself* which harbors the seed for the internal dissolution or loss of meaning in rationalization. The second is that Weber does not see the opportunity for a form of secularized communicative ethic that is liberated from its foundation in religious salvation, as is the case with science and autonomous art. Weber maintains that ethics must remain linked to its religious foundation in order to talk about a meaningful rationalization. This is why Habermas introduces communicative ethics, which in the German philosopher Karl-Otto Apel's version of this, will be treated in Chapter 4.

Weber's Theory of the Rationalization of Law

According to Weber's theory, law plays a similar role to the Protestant ethic in the institutionalization of goal-oriented rational action in modern society.

Law serves to create firm ground for exercising goal-oriented rational action within the capitalist social system. As the Protestant ethic loses its importance as the foundation for the ethic of calling, law steps in to guarantee goal-oriented rational action. In this way, law, in Weber's theory, plays the same double role as ethics previously did. Law, in economics and administration, should fill the meaning vacuum that was created due to the increasing marginalization of the Protestant calling ethic; but this can only occur if law evades the same normative degradation which was the fate of the Protestant ethic. Weber tried to solve this problem by freeing modern law from the cultural value sphere of moral-practical rationality and instead placing it in the sphere of cognitive-instrumental rationality.[29] The problem that then arises for Weber is how law is able to give goal-oriented rational action the value and normative foundation which it previously obtained through the Protestant calling ethic.[30] This can also be called the problem of the legitimation of law. Law should be able to be justified, but such a justification requires a form of rational agreement.

In Weber's positivist legal theory, the issue of the legitimation of law is posed as a question about the use of law. Since Weber, this conception has been used almost as a slogan in the title of Niklas Luhmann's book *Legitimation durch Verfahren*.[31] What is implied here is keeping to particular dictums, processes and procedures when applying the law in courts. Alf Ross expresses himself in much the same way in his book on legal philosophy *Ret og Retfærdighed* (Law and Justice):

> As we have seen, the ideas of justice and equality dissolve in the entirely formal demand that concrete decisions are presented as the use of a general rule, *regardless of which rule it is*. Justice is the correct use of rules as opposed to arbitrariness.[32]

In this conception, all traces of normativity as rational agreement have disappeared. Legitimacy collapses into legality; there is no possibility of distinguishing between them.

The legitimacy of rational supremacy rests, according to Weber, on 'the belief in the legality of a given order and the belief that those who are called to exercise authority have a right to do so'.[33] The problem, however, is how legality receives its credibility, as legality only means accordance with existing legislation, and it is precisely this which is to be legitimated. This is totally tautological.[34]

Sociologically, this contradiction is resolved, according to Weber, by what could be called 'a secondary traditionalism'.[35] The empirical 'legitimacy' of the 'rational' order is, according to Weber, built upon a '*Fügsamkeit*', a 'compliance' with the customary, the familiar, that which is passed on through socialization and that which is continuously repeated.[36] The contradiction in the rationalization of law is, according to Weber, that the more law is rationalized, the more distant the rational core of law becomes from those affected. Weber goes so far as to say that modern man has less *insight* into the rationality of his life order than 'the wild' men.[37] The universalization of knowledge leads sociologically not to greater insight into the connections within the social order, but rather to the opposite, according to Weber.[38]

Modern secondary traditionalism differentiates itself from the traditionalism of 'wild' people, in that modern secondary traditionalism is built on a belief that it is possible to put forward a rational foundation for a legal order, and that therefore it is possible to make calculations of rational action in relation to this order. What is presented here, however, is a sociology of law theory which clearly can indicate that a problem of legitimacy exists, but it cannot solve it. Belief in legality is, as Habermas notes, *not* an independent legitimation type.[39] But in Weber's theory it can appear to be so.

In that Weber stands by his positivistic legal conception, he can entirely lay the rationalization of law in the cognitive value sphere. Rationalization of law, according to Weber, means primarily processing the formal qualities of the law through the professionalization of judicial institutions; analytical systematization of the law, as well as the above mentioned process of turning the issue of the legitimacy of the foundations of law into a question about the procedure whereby legislation, is adopted. In this way it is not just possible for Weber to push aside moral-practical rationality, but it also comes to be portrayed in his theory as a weakening of formal law's rationality.[40]

The Contradiction in Weber's Theory of Modernity

This leads to a contradiction in Weber's assessment of action rationality in modern society. On the one hand, Weber *regrets* in *The Protestant Ethic and the Spirit of Capitalism* that the Protestant ethic in politics and economics degenerates into a utilitarian action orientation. On the other hand, he tones down the moral-practical dimension in his legal theory. Weber in this way opens up his theory for a reduction of law to a steering instrument for goal-oriented rational action's dominance in economics and administration. In Weber's theory, modernization and rationalization are identified as the dominance of goal-oriented rational action in economic and bureaucratic institutions.

This contradiction between, on the one hand, regretting the dissolution of the Protestant ethic and, on the other hand, diminishing ethics as a theoretical issue, is the point at which Habermas takes up his critique of Weber. According to Habermas, this contradiction arises due to Weber having a too one-sided understanding of social rationalization, one which excludes the moral-practical dimension. It is against this background that Habermas attempts to present a more differentiated conception of action in his theory of communicative action which includes both goal-oriented rational action and communicative action.[41]

After the religious world views have been broken down according to Weber's socio-religious analysis, Habermas sees it as an open empirical question as to why the three above mentioned cultural rationality complexes which have become differentiated, have not been equally institutionalized and, in an equivalent manner, determine the communicative practice of daily life.[42] According to Habermas, Weber has already answered this question by viewing the rationalization of society from a goal-oriented rationality perspective. Habermas criticizes this fundamental understanding of Weber, and thereby mades it the point of departure in analyzing the concept of communicative action. In this way, Habermas opens the way for a more open understanding of modern society than the pessimistic understanding expressed in Weber's theory.

Two Versions of Weber's Theory of Action

In the opening of *Economy and Society*, Weber defines his theory of action:

> We shall speak of 'action' insofar as the acting individual attaches a subjective meaning to his behavior – be it overt or covert, omission or acquiescence.[43]

It is clear from this definition that meaning is what is important for a behaviour to become an action. Habermas agrees with Weber that it is meaning which is important in defining an action. The problem then becomes how an action obtains meaning. This is where the conflict between Weber and Habermas lies.

To Weber, meaning is first and foremost bound to that which the individual attaches to the action. In this connection, Weber has four conceptions of action; goal-oriented rationality, value rationality, the affectual and the traditional.[44] Weber defines goal-oriented rationality in the following way:

> Action is instrumentally rational (*zweckrational*) when the end, the means and the secondary results are all rationally taken into account and weighed. This involves rational consideration of alternative means to the end, of the relation of the end to the secondary consequences, and finally of the relative importance of different possible ends. Determination of action either in affectual or in traditional terms is thus incompatible with this type. Choice between alternative and conflicting ends and results may well be determined in a value rational manner. In that case, action is instrumentally rational only in respect to the choice of means. On the other hand, the actor may, instead of deciding between alternative and conflicting ends in terms of a rational orientation to a system of values, simply take them as given subjective wants and arrange them in a scale of consciously assessed relative urgency. ... Value rational action may thus have various different relations to the instrumentally rational action. From the latter point of view, however, value rationality is always irrational. Indeed, the more the value to which action is oriented is elevated to the status of an absolute value, the more 'irrational' in the sense the corresponding action is. For, the more unconditionally the actor devotes himself to this value for its ow sake, to pure sentiment or beauty, to absolute goodness, or devotion to duty, the less is he influenced by considerations of the consequences of his actions. The orientation of action wholly to the rational achievement of ends without relation to fundamental values is, to be sure, only a limiting.[45]

The four conceptions of action are arranged in a hierarchy based on their degree of rationality. Goal-oriented rationality stands highest because it rationally evaluates the ends, means, values and (side)effects of an action.[46]

Habermas, however, believes that it is also possible to find fragments of another type of theory of action in Weber, in which Weber should differentiate between an action based on an interest and an action based on normative consent.[47] Habermas believes that this differentiation comes to expression in Weber; on the one hand, in the economy and on the other, in an acknowledged legal order. Habermas does not feel that Weber has adequately developed a conception of action that takes normative consent into account. This was also shown in the discussion of the legitimation problem in Weber's legal theory.

Habermas utilizes the distinction between interest and consent to develop an alternative conception of action. Goal-oriented rational action is interest based and is oriented towards reaching some defined goal, or result-based on adequate rational means, and takes into consideration the effects of different possible actions. Such a result-oriented theory is termed an instrumental action by Habermas when it follows technical rules for action and is evaluated by the effectiveness of an intervention in a context of circumstances or events. A result-oriented strategy is called a strategic action when it follows rules which build upon a rational choice, and effectiveness is evaluated by the influence the action has on the decisions of a rational counterpart. Instrumental action can be attached to social interaction; strategic action represents in itself a social action. Habermas contrasts this with communicative action.[48]

In communicative action, the action plans of the actors involved are not coordinated by egocentric result calculations, but from mutual understanding. In communicative or understanding-oriented action, the actors involved are not primarily oriented towards obtaining a result by seeing their counterparts as competitors, but rather are concerned with pursuing their goals, taking into consideration the plans of each other on the basis of a *collective* assessment of their situation. The central characteristic of this understanding-oriented action is that through communication a common horizon of understanding for action can be created.

Communicative Action

The point of departure for this concept of understanding, according to Habermas, is the pre-theoretical knowledge that it is possible for a speaker to intuitively know when he is trying to influence others, when he is trying to achieve mutual understanding and finally, when such mutual understanding is successful.[49] Habermas's project can be characterized as an attempt to explicitly clarify this intuitive knowledge. This mutual understanding cannot exclusively refer to intuitive consent because it must be possible to express it in order to examine the content of the common understanding. Mutual understanding must then be built on a rational foundation. Only in this way can one differentiate between forced consent and freely acknowledged consent. This is where language enters Habermas's theory, as mutual understanding can only be expressed and tested through language.

In this context, Habermas presents his thesis that mutual understanding is the innate goal or *telos* of human language.[50] Or, put in other words: human language aims at mutual understanding. What is meant here is that when language is properly used in agreement with intuitive knowledge, as noted above, it aims at mutual understanding. This is an anthropological postulate which has deep roots both in the Greek and Judeo-Christian tradition. In this context it can be helpful to recall Aristotle's definition of the human in the beginning of his *Politics*. The human, according to Aristotle, is the only living being possessing *logos*.[51] *Logos* in Greek means both speech and reason, as reason comes to expression in speech. One can say that Habermas wants to return to the original understanding of speech, as it was, for example, formulated by Aristotle, but which also is found in the wider tradition of Greek philosophy and political culture. When I speak of returning to an original understanding of language, this is connected to language being instrumentalized through the process of cultural rationalization. What is meant here is that language is used for something other than its essential definition, namely, as an instrument to dominate other people's ways of acting. Such use of language is a misuse of language. According to Habermas, it is precisely this type of use and misuse of language which is found in goal-oriented rational action.

To substantiate this thesis, Habermas must show that understanding-oriented language use is language's original modus, upon which instrumental use of language is a parasite that corrodes language's original meaning – to reach mutual understanding.[52] This could also be expressed as Habermas wishing to criticize the use or misuse of language which, along with goal-oriented rational action, has become dominant in our society. To do this it is not adequate merely to refer to antique or early modern philosophy. As mentioned, Aristotle could give an anthropologically bound definition of original language, but he cannot give a critique of goal-oriented rational action due to the simple fact that this form of rationality was not dominant in the Greek city-states. It is also first in this century's modern linguistic philosophy that this issue is taken up. In this context, Habermas builds primarily on the speech act theories of John L. Austin and John R. Searle.[53]

The fundamental thesis of these speech act theories is that there is a direct connection between speech and action; that one can act through speech. To speak is to act. Austin differentiates between three aspects of a speech act: locution, illocution and perlocution. Locution refers to the content or matter of the speech act. This can be a sentence such as 'The tree is green'. By illocution, the speaker acts, in that he says something. An example of this would be 'T said to H: 'the tree is green''. In perlocution, the speaker aims at having an effect on the listener. An example of this would be 'To make H happy, T said: 'the tree is green''. The three aspects of speech actions can be summarized in the following way. In locution, something is *said*. In illocution, *action* is taken, in that something is said. In perlocution, an *effect on the listener is intended*, by acting, in that something is said.[54]

In Austin's theory, illocution is a self-sufficient act that serves to communicate a particular message that the listener can understand and accept. Self-sufficient should be understood as the intention that that which is said directly appears in the meaning of what is said. In illocution it is the meaning of that which is said, that is to say locution, which is decisive. The situation with perlocution is different. Here there is an external consideration which the speech act must serve. In the example given above, it was to make the listener happy. Perlocution is thus not a self-sufficient or autonomous speech act. It is rather a *means* to obtain a goal which is established outside the speech act. Therefore, perlocution or result-oriented speech acts, according to Habermas, are not original speech acts. In result-oriented speech action, illocutionary communication is subsumed or subordinated to externally defined goals which have a contingent or arbitrary relation to the meaning of what is said (locution).[55] Perlocution is a strategic speech act, where one communicates with reservation. The reservation is that communication should serve an externally defined goal which establishes the true meaning of the speech act and which must not be disclosed. If the strategic goal is disclosed, the meaning of the sentence crumbles and the asymmetry between the speaker and the listener is exposed.

An extension of the examples given above is a sentence which could look like: 'I tell you now that the tree is green to make you happy'. Such a sentence would not bring happiness because it discloses that there is not a free and equal relationship between the speaker and listener. Language is used as an instrument by the speaker. Illocution, however, is a direct communicative relationship between the speaker and listener. In this form of interaction, all participants can present their individual plans to each other and therefore *without reservation* pursue their illocutionary goals. It is this form of communication that Habermas calls *communicative action.*[56] In contrast to this, Habermas calls interaction, in which at least one of the actors through his speech acts seeks to evoke perlocutionary effects in his conversation partners, linguistically mediated *strategic action.*[57]

Meaning and Validity

The question now is what conditions the communicatively reached consensus must meet in order to serve to coordinate action. Habermas's answer here is that we understand a speech act when we know what makes it acceptable.[58] There is then an inner connection between the meaning and validity of an understanding-oriented speech act. A sentence could be: 'I urge you not to smoke in this room'. The speaker can only *motivate* the listener to *rationally* accept his proposal when he can give a rational reason for the connection between the meaning and validity of the proposal.[59] The point is not that the validity in itself in a proposal gives the proposal meaning, but rather the *possibility* to give *rational reasons* for the validity of a proposal. The listener is motivated by the possibility of the rational reasoning, and not by the proposal itself. In this, communicative action differentiates itself from strategic action. The given sentence can also be expressed as a strategic speech act. It can, for example, be directed at passengers on an aeroplane about to land. Also in this case there can be a rational reason for the proposal, but acknowledgement of the proposal's validity is not just based upon the passengers acknowledging the rational reasoning of the proposal. Acknowledgement in this case is also based on what Habermas calls external understanding or contingent empirically-oriented potential for sanctions which are associated with the speech act.[60] Or, expressed in other words, acknowledgement of the utterance in the case above is built upon the fact that the flight attendant has the authority to apply sanctions against a passenger who may have understood the rational reasons for the proposal, but still continues to smoke. In this case, motivation in the final instance rests on power, and not reason. In communicative action, motivation takes place solely through reason. In communicative action, validity claims are *open to criticism*; they can be questioned.[61] In strategic action, validity claims cannot be criticized. It is not the case that communicative action is rational and strategic action is irrational. Strategic action can also be rationally based. The issue is that communicative action is exclusively based upon what Habermas calls communicative reason, by which he means that the meaning of a speech act is connected with validity claims which can be justified and also criticized.[62] In strategic action there is no integral connection between meaning and validity; strategic action is maintained through power, which can be rationally justified. But the validity of this justification cannot be questioned or criticized. Therefore strategic action in the final instance is not communicative in character.

Classification and Validity Claims

After delimiting communicative action in relation to other forms of action, it can be differentiated from other different types of action and their respective validity claims. Here Habermas differentiates between three ideal types of speech acts; the regulative, the constative, and the expressive. Regulative speech acts revolve around social relations where what is examined is *the correct* in a given situation.[63] Constative speech acts take up matters in the world in which the *truth* in a particular situation is under examination. Expressive speech acts deal with subjective experiences where the *authenticity* of a particular expression is under scrutiny. The three ideal typical speech acts are related to the social world, the objective world and the subjective world, respectively, and these relations are linked to three validity claims: correctness, truth and authenticity. Habermas then uses these three types of speech acts to create three ideal types of linguistically mediated interaction or communicative action; regulative speech acts are paired with norm regulated action, constative action with the 'conversation' and expressive speech acts with dramaturgical action.[64]

Based on this classification, it should, according to Habermas, be possible at the ideal typical level to differentiate between on the one hand, strategic action and on the other, communicative action, and subsequently between different forms of communicative action. Such a theory of linguistic action concerning the importance and use of language is called 'formal pragmatics' by Habermas.

Formal and Empirical Pragmatics

The classifications of formal pragmatics forms the foundation for empirically analyzing different forms of speech acts. In this case, Habermas speaks of 'empirical pragmatics'. With empirical pragmatics, Habermas hopes to soften up the ideal types of formal pragmatics on a number of points.[65] The three most important modifications should be named here. First, the postulate of formal pragmatics – that the linguistic utterance covers the meaning of the content of the utterance – falls. Second, language to an increasing degree is consigned to its context. Third, the sharp distinction between understanding and result-oriented action is softened.[66]

These modifications do not alter the original intention, that formal pragmatics should serve in finding the rational foundation for linguistic communication in observable daily life's confusing complexity. In this connection, Habermas names three areas where formal pragmatics can be of importance with regard to clarifying the rational foundation of the process of understanding.

First, formal pragmatics can give principal insight into the many different speech acts. What is meant by 'speech acts' is the special use of language dependent on what context the language use is part of. Such insight is learnt through socialization. But when there is confusion in language games, it can be helpful in principle to be able to differentiate between different language games.

Formal pragmatics can also give insight into that which Habermas calls systematically distorted communication.[67] Systematically distorted communication is labelled by Habermas as a pathological form of communication. Pathological traits in communication, according to Habermas, are a result of the combination of result-oriented and understanding-oriented action. In masked strategic action, one participant holds to his result orientation while letting the others believe that the conditions for communicative actions are reached. In as much as this is a consciously masked strategic action, one can speak of manipulation. There can also be a form of unconscious masking of conflicts which psychoanalysis explains in terms of defense mechanisms and which leads to the destruction of communication both on the inner psychic and interpersonal levels.[68] In such a situation, at least one participant does not realize that he is acting strategically, but rather believes he is acting communicatively.

The third capacity of formal pragmatics is that its pure types of linguistically mediated interaction make it possible to highlight the aspects under which social action incarnates different forms of knowledge.[69] In contrast to Weber's theory of action, Habermas's theory of communicative action is not fixated on goal-oriented rationality as the only aspect by which action can be criticized and improved. In Habermas's theory there is a far more nuanced conception of action rationality, which will be briefly summarized here.[70]

Goal-oriented or teleological action is evaluated from the activity's perspective. These actions contain a *technical* or *strategic* use of knowledge, which can be criticized from a truth criterion, and can be improved through a growth in empirical-theoretical knowledge. Such knowledge is accumulated in technologies and strategies.

Constative speech acts bring knowledge to expression in conversations which can be criticized based on a truth criterion. When wide disagreement arises concerning the truth of a statement, the conversation is shifted to theoretical discourse. When empirical knowledge is systematically tested, knowledge can be accumulated in the form of theories.

Norm-regulated action comprises moral-practical knowledge. Moral-practical knowledge can be tested by the application of correctness. A claim of correctness can be tested by way of discourse. When regulative language use is damaged, norms can be tested in practical discourse. In moral practical argumentation, participants can test the correctness of a particular action in relation to a given norm, and on the next level, the correctness of the norm can be tested. This knowledge is collected and given in the form of legal and moral conceptions.

Dramaturgical action contains knowledge about the action's own internal subjective world. These expressions can be criticized as untruthful, either consciously or unconsciously. Unconscious self-deception can be discovered in the psychoanalytic, therapeutic conversation. Expressive knowledge can be expressed in the form of values which have to do with needs, desires, feelings, etc. Criteria of value can in part develop through interpretive conversation and in part in objective forms, such as works of art.

Action Rationalities and the Life World

Habermas's creation of theories of action, types of knowledge and argumentation forms is inspired by Weber's conception that European modernity is marked by differentiation in the forms of science, morality and art, which bring in different forms of institutionalized everyday action that pressure and rationalize previous traditionally informed action orientation. The theory of communicative action offers the opportunity to give a more nuanced picture of this rationalization than the selective rationalization which is found in Weber's theory of goal-oriented rational action.[71] According to Habermas, this is because in the theory of rational action, it is just not possible to state that the different forms of speech acts contain knowledge of an explicitly rational character; but that they also play out themselves based on this background knowledge in what Habermas calls the 'life world'. By this Habermas means that a statement cannot exclusively be understood in itself; it must be understood in the light of the implicit knowledge which is rooted in the life world. This fundamental background knowledge has three characteristics, according to Habermas.[72] First, there is an implicit knowledge which cannot be expressed. Second, this knowledge is holistically structured in the sense that it builds upon an internal reference and only refers to itself. Third, this knowledge cannot be utilized, as it in its entirety it cannot be made conscious or brought into doubt. It only comes partially forward when certain fundamental postulates are brought into doubt.

Communicative action plays itself out with the life world as its reference point. The life world in Habermas's theory is a complimentary concept to communicative action.[73] This is a transcendental philosophical concept which is introduced as a foundation and reference point for mutual understanding.[74] Life world, in this context, refers to an implicit knowledge of an holistic character which in its entirety is not open for utilization. It is a reference point for understanding. As such, the concept serves on an abstract ideal typical level to formulate a conception of society from a pure participant/actor perspective.[75] Society here is understood as a communicative corporation or a cognitive cooperative within the life world's frame of reference.[76]

This conception of society, according to Habermas, is based on three fictions.[77] The first is that action is autonomous. The second is the independence of culture. The third is the independence of communication. These three fictions cannot be sustained, according to Habermas, because society cannot reproduce itself exclusively through communicative action.[78] Society is equally reproduced through functional systems. What is primarily referred to here is the material reproduction of society through capitalist market production and the state's steering of society through bureaucracy. There is, according to Habermas, a *limit* to the understanding of society from the communicative perspective. It is equally important, he believes, to see society from a system integrative perspective. According to Habermas, society must be seen both from an action and a systemic perspective. This correlates to an internal and external perspective on society. In Habermas's theory, the action perspective is the primary perspective, and it is the limitations of this perspective that lead to the system perspective.

The point is that social life cannot entirely be understood directly. For the individual, society is reproduced as an independent entity in the form of social institutions which make their own demands on individuals. This is exactly what Hegel means, as noted earlier, in his legal theory when he states that life is *mediated* through society's *institutions*. It is in this connection that power and domination come to play a decisive role. In the following discussion, this issue will be examined with special weight placed on modern politics and administration.

2 Modern Politics and Administration

Modern Politics

In the following pages we will look closely at how modern society is institutionally expressed in politics and administration. The reason for this is to present the institutional setting for the administrator's ethical dilemma.

Modern society has been a long time in coming, from its rise in the late Middle Ages through to the present. There are a number of high points in this rise, such as the Renaissance and the Reformation. It is, however, the French Revolution which marks the final breakthrough of modern society. This is because the French Revolution created an entirely new understanding of society. With the French Revolution, politics became the foundation of modern society. It is here that democracy comes onto the agenda of history.

Until the French Revolution, European society was primarily a hierarchically composed estate society. The prince or king was the head of society, and all other members of society were subjects of the prince, each born into a particular estate. The dominance of the prince was theologically and metaphysically justified in the form of God-given power. In this way, society as a totality became a metaphysically justified order which comprised part of a larger, religiously founded cosmological order. Christianity was the great guarantor of the sanctity of this social order. It was from the theological interpretation of Christianity that the social order's basic norms were derived. In the Middle Ages, the prince had his power symbolically conveyed through the Pope. In this way the authority of the prince was ultimately secured by its derivation from the God-given order. Max Weber called this type of authority traditional authority, and a society based on this type of authority, a traditional society.

In Weber's interpretation of Western society, the social order of traditional society was eroded by the secularization of the forms of religious understanding. The European Reformation movements of the 1500s are of decisive importance here, as they set the individual in the centre. Each individual became an independent, legitimate person in his relationship with God. It meant that the relationship to God no longer had to be mediated through the institution of the Church. The Church thereby lost its sacred aura. This also meant that the church as an institution could no longer stand as the guarantor of the social order. The holy was no longer mediated through a hierarchical social and institutional relationship.

This historical process must be seen in connection with the separation of society as an independent sphere which gradually separates from the religious sphere. Society begins to become worldly and modern. Here the problem arises as to how is it possible to independently justify society without reference to the religiously informed metaphysic. Luther solved this problem through his 'doctrine of two regimes', which proposed that the prince was placed here by God to rule over the temporal world. In this way Luther's theology acts as a transition from Middle Age theology to the modern secularized understanding of society. On the one side, Luther's theology sets off the worldly as an independent area. On the other side, Luther maintains that the prince's power is theologically founded. This form of theological justification of princely power comes to form the background in the 1700s for Enlightenment philosophy's independent natural law oriented justification of power in the worldly society. The theological justification of the worldly society hereby loses its meaning.

The central issue in the Enlightenment philosophy of the 1700s with regard to the relationship between rulers and the ruled can be summarized in Enlightenment philosophy's three models: natural law, the social pact and the ruler's contract.[79]

Natural law is based on the conception that there are some universal rights which are valid for all people and should be the foundation for the law in society. Natural law is thus a critical way of evaluating the laws of society. According to this theory, laws are only legitimate if they are in accordance with natural law. By reference to natural law, demands can be made on rights in society. In the first case, natural law is about the right to protect life and property. But natural law can also be expanded to cover a number of other areas, such as the right to express oneself freely in speech and writing.

The social contract is based upon the idea that people, who in the state of nature are understood as isolated monads, have a reasoned interest in grouping together in society in which they can implement laws derived from natural law, which among other things can comprise the above mentioned rights to protection of life, property, freedom of expression, etc.

When a society based on the rule of law is established, the members of society can choose a ruler, who, through a ruler's contract is obligated to protect and defend the legally enshrined rights.

Natural law, the social contract and the ruler's contract were the key words in the literary protest against the absolutist regime in France in the 1700s. But as to the fundamental conception of which rights society was formed to have recognized, and which the prince was enthroned to protect, opinions divided. Two opposing interpretations of natural law were found in the Estate assembly of 1789, which comprised two groups who formed a tactical alliance in the years 1787-1788 to defend the rights of the French population.

One group essentially defended privilege and the aristocracy. In this interpretation, it was the role of the king to ensure that the French estates' traditional and differing intra-estate rights were respected, both in relation to the monarchy and between the estates. This orientation wished to restore the old estate society. The interest here was to prevent the first and second estates, the ecclesiastic and noble estates, respectively, from having to pay tax.

The other interpretation of natural law, which was put forward by enlightenment philosophers and the defenders of the third estate, interpreted natural law in a universalistic manner. Based on this interpretation, the prince was obligated to abolish all traditional estate privileges. This understanding of the social contract and the ruler's contract led to the doctrine of popular sovereignty.

According to the doctrine of popular sovereignty, the source of all power in society ultimately lies with the people, who through a collective decision created society. Therefore, according to this interpretation, it is only the people who have the right to decide how society should be organized.

At the end of the 1700s, two interpretations of the doctrine of popular sovereignty emerged. One interpretation, the 'constitutional interpretation' posited that the sovereign people, through the adoption of a constitution, establish certain guiding principles for the political process and where the natural rights, which also can be called human rights, are given a positive legal status as constitutionally secured rights for the citizenry. By adopting such a constitution, a threefold division of power would occur. The doctrine of division of powers was known from the writings of Montesquieu and Locke and from the declarations and constitutions of the states' and federal government of the newly established United States of America. According to the doctrine of the division of power, power should be divided along legislative, executive and judicial lines. In this way popular sovereignty is also split into three. This should prohibit the power of the people from being exercised in a new tyrannical form.

According to the other interpretation, inspired by Jean-Jacques Rousseau, popular sovereignty cannot be split. Popular sovereignty, in this case, always stands above the tripartite division of power.

The French Revolution

It was these thoughts which formed the background for the French Revolution. On 5 May, 1789 Louis XVI officially opened the Estate Assembly in Versailles with the intention of creating new taxes. It rapidly became clear that what at first looked like a political and economic crisis was really a crisis of legitimacy, where supporters of a new constitution, primarily the representatives of the third estate, presented a different legitimacy, one based on the rights of the nation. In an action-packed series of events over the course of several months, the third estate succeeded in expanding the Estate Assembly both in terms of their own representation into forming a national assembly, which soon became a constitution creating assembly. This set the stage for a radical break with feudal society's religious and metaphysically based monarchy and the establishment of the fundamental institution of modern society, the democratic political institution. The final legitimacy collapse occurred on 17 June, 1789, when the Third Estate unilaterally established a national assembly. In the famous Tennis Court Oath, which was given a few days later, the new national assembly vowed to remain in assembly until 'the kingdom's constitution is established and rested on a solid foundation'.[80] To legitimate this task, the national assembly bestowed upon itself the status of a *constitutional* assembly.

In the report of the committee established to prepare work on the constitution which was presented on 9 July, the ideas on a declaration of human rights were formalized: 'For a constitution to be good, it must be based on human rights and naturally protect them. In order to prepare a constitution one must know which rights natural justice ascribes to all individuals. One must bear in mind the principles which should be the foundation of every form of society'. Therefore the constitution must 'begin with a declaration of humans' natural and inalienable rights'.[81] In the report, the fundamental principles of the new legitimacy were stated: 'We believe that a constitution is nothing more than a set and established order for a way of governing; that this order cannot exist if it is not supported by fundamental rules created by the power of a nation's formal and free association'.[82]

The constitutive national assembly began its legislative work by discussing the formulation of a declaration of natural and inalienable human rights. This work culminated with the adoption on 26 August of the 'Declaration of Human and Citizens' Rights'.

From a philosophical and political science perspective, the period from the time when the third estate constituted itself as a national assembly and founding power to the adoption of the declaration of human and citizen's rights is of exceptional interest. It is during this period that the transformation of French society took place, which justifies the label revolution. In this period the religious and metaphysical basis of the monarchy fell. It lost its legitimacy. The problem which remained, however, was what would take the place of the religious and metaphysical justification of power. Initially a power vacuum developed, a power nothingness. It is this nothingness which is central, as it marks the core or centre of modern society.

Modern society, in distinction to all other known forms of society, is based on a nothingness or empty space of power, as expressed by the French philosopher Claude Lefort. The problem then is how the new social order can be constituted. In this context, Lefort highlights the transition from the discourse of power to the power of discourse.[83] In the feudal order, the prince represented the discourse of power. When the prince spoke, it was power speaking. Power was therefore decided beforehand. With the revolutionary transformation, speech itself came to constitute power. The representatives in the national assembly had to constitute or create the new social order through their speech. Discourse, argumentation and conversation took on an entirely new importance. The social order constituted – through the speech and conversation of the deputies – a reference in and to itself. Society then became self-referential. It can no longer refer to a preordained metaphysically secured social order. The social order had to constitute itself by linguistic reference to society itself.

This agrees with Habermas's interpretation of modern society as it was presented in the previous chapter.

In this constitution, political or state citizens were created in the sense that it is the citizens who decide as humans or citizens in society's political decisions. The declaration of human and citizen's rights should be understood in this context. In the declaration, a systematic presentation of the foundations of modern democratic society is given.

The Declaration of Human and Citizen's Rights

In the Declaration, the constituting of the political collectivity in society is expressed. The decisive break with the religiously and metaphysically based power (the king) in feudal society is expressed already in Article 1, where it states:

> Humans are born and remain free and equal in rights. Social difference can only be justified based on the common good.

This article introduces the two fundamental concepts in the new constitution, freedom and equality. Freedom is universal. No person can in principle assert that he has a greater right to freedom than another person. Next, all persons are in principle equal in rights. What is meant here is that no person in principle can assert a right over another person. Each person has the right to have their rights respected.

Article 2 then elaborates on the goal of the political union, when it states, 'the goal of any political union is to preserve the natural and inalienable human rights'. Then follows the specification of human rights as the right to 'freedom, property, security and resistance to oppression'.

Article 3 declares that the fundamental political union is the nation. What is meant here is the political collectivity which is precisely constituted as a linguistic collectivity. The point is, and it is stated in the following sentence, that no union, no individual can exercise authority which does not stem from the nation, which is synonymous with the linguistic political collectivity. It is precisely this thought we found formulated above in Habermas's theory of communicative action.

After dealing with the political collectivity in the first three articles,

articles 4-9 take up freedom as the political collectivity's primary dimension. Freedom, in Article 4, is defined in the following way:

> Freedom is being allowed to do anything that does not harm another. Therefore, the exercise of every individual's natural rights is only limited by the allowance of all other members of society to exercise the same rights. These rights can only be established through law.

Freedom is defined negatively in the Declaration. Any action which does not harm another is permissible. This, in principle, grants the same freedom for all members of society. But in order to realize this freedom, actions taken at the expense of others must be prohibited. In other words, a limit to freedom must be set, which is precisely the limiting of actions which impair the freedom of others. This limit can only be established through law. This is stated in Article 5:

> The law is only allowed to prohibit actions which harm society. Everything that is not forbidden by law cannot be obstructed, and no one can be forced to do what it does not dictate.

This article specifies the role of law. The law should protect freedom. In the article, the collectivity decides where freedom should prevail as a society. In the Declaration, there is a close connection between freedom and society. This is further refined in the second part of the Article, where it states that it is only in law that limits can be set on freedom. This is elaborated in Article 6:

> The law expresses the general will (*la volonté générale*). All citizens have the right to, either personally or through their representatives, take part in its formulation; it shall be the same for all, whether it protects or punishes. All citizens in its eyes are equal, shall have equal access to all posts of honor, public offices and positions, based on their abilities and with no other criteria than their virtues and talents.

The law is the expression of the 'general will'. This '*volonté générale*' is again understood through freedom. Precisely through the postulate of freedom is it possible to speak of a general will, precisely that which secures the freedom of all members of society. Therefore, it is consistently reiterated in that which follows that all members of society have a right to participate in the legislative process. In this way, all citizens have the right to state how their freedom is threatened by other members of society. It is a similar thought which Habermas formulates in his idea of communicative action. In this way, the freedoms of belief and expression take a central place in the Declaration. This is formulated in Articles 10 and 11. Article 10 takes up freedom of belief:

> No one, based on their beliefs, not even religious beliefs, should have grounds for fear, so long as the exercise of these beliefs do not disturb the lawfully established social order.

This article deals with general freedom of belief, and hereunder freedom of religion. No restrictions may be placed on what society's members may think or believe so long as they do not affect the same freedoms of other members of society. This is why it is mentioned that the exercise of freedom of belief may not disturb the lawfully established social order. In reality, this article expresses the final break with religious and metaphysically based (monarchical) power. The social order can no longer be justified in terms of a preordained religion or metaphysic, and no person can prescribe a particular belief or religious faith. The social order can only be expressed in law. This is elaborated in Article 11:

> The free exchange of ideas and beliefs is a right dear to people. Therefore, each citizen can speak, write and print freely, under the proviso of responsibility in the case of abuse of this freedom in accordance with the law.

Freedom of expression is central to modern democratic society because each member of society, through free expression has the opportunity to participate in defining the limitations of freedom. Counterfactually, it could be stated that if there was not full freedom of expression, there would be no freedom, because each individual would not have the opportunity to state when his freedom is threatened. It is precisely this thought we found in Habermas's theory of communicative action, and which he also treats in detail in his most recent major work *Faktiztät und Geltung.*[84] Each member of society must have the possibility to participate in the determination of the limits of freedom, so that the law can be an expression of the general will.[85]

Article 11 establishes a transition in the constituting process. The first

10 articles deal with human rights, and how humans together constitute a society which is based on freedom. In Article 11, the constituting process is culminated, in so far as in this article there is no longer talk exclusively of humans, but also of citizens. Article 12 can therefore be seen as the first article on the constitution of bourgeois society:

> The securing of human and citizen's rights requires a public power, this power is therefore instituted for the advantage of all (*instituée pour l'advantage de tous*) and not for the special use (*l'utilité particulière*) of those in whom it is vested.

The problem is to secure the freedom rights of humans and citizens. Man has been incarnated as citizen and his freedom, which is defined in Article 11, is now to be secured as the freedom rights of the citizen. To do this, a public power is required. This power is of an entirely different character than the religiously and metaphysically based (monarchical) power of feudal society. This new power is '*instituée*', it is institutionalized to the advantage of all, and not for the use of those to whom it is invested.

The following articles, Articles 13-16, deal with defining this public power. Only the most important points will be highlighted here.

Article 13 contains the important principle that citizens will contribute to the public power and administration in accordance with their means. In the following two articles, it is stated that the citizens shall have the power to decide the amount and purpose of these funds, and that it should be possible to control each administrator's exercise of authority. Article 16 defines the tripartite division of power as fundamental to the legitimacy of the constitution. In the last article, it is stated that the right to property is 'inviolable and holy' and that a public authority can only expropriate property with the payment of full compensation.

Modern Democratic Society

The declaration of human and citizen's rights during the French Revolution marks the final breakthrough of modern society. This is an historical break, which symbolically can be portrayed as the transition from a triangle to a circle. In traditional feudal society, the religious and metaphysically based power is concentrated at the top of society. Through this hierarchical structuring of society, power is infused from top to bottom. Each person is born into an estate in which he must obey a predetermined power. In this conception of society, the individual possesses no authority to participate in the ruling of society.

The breakthrough of modern society in the French Revolution broke radically with this conception of society. Modern society empties power of its predetermined content. Social power is then constituted here and now through discussion among equal partners. Freedom of expression and publicity hereby become decisive for modern society. Modern society's new centre becomes the public space in which the citizen can freely express himself. Through this, the political is created in modern democratic society. It is this understanding of modern society that is presented in the Declaration of Human and Citizen's Rights.

This is an ideal type which has to be modified in two ways. The first is that it must be recognized that politics is usually fused with particular social interests and that in this way takes on a strategic character. Second, the ideal or typical picture of politics must be made concrete in a differentiated picture of the institutions of modern society. These two modifications do not, however, disturb the principal understanding of modern society as it is presented in the Declaration.

With regard to the first point, the form of modification is identical to that which was taken up in the above discussion of Habermas's theory of communicative action. There it was shown that strategic action in linguistic theoretical terms has to be understood in terms of communicative action. Habermas has also treated this issue in detail from a political theory perspective with his concept of 'deliberative politics' which he develops in *Faktizität und Geltung*.[86] By deliberative politics Habermas means, as the word deliberate implies, a politics based on consideration, advice, consultation and discussion. With the concept of deliberate politics, Habermas wants to take into consideration the manifold forms of communication, in which a common will is not only established through an ethical argumentation, but also through compromise building upon an evening out of interest conflicts based on goal-oriented rationality.[87]

With regard to the second point, the differentiation of the institutions of modern society does not denigrate the principal understanding of this social formation. On the contrary, differentiation must be understood on the basis of these principal definitions. It is in this context that the modern administrator comes into the picture.

Weber's Theory of Modern Bureaucracy

All currently known, highly evolved cultures have been steered through an administration. It is not, therefore, administration which characterizes modern society. That which especially characterizes modern administration is its rational character. It is first and foremost Max Weber who has highlighted this. Therefore, Max Weber's theory of modern bureaucracy is unavoidable if one wants to understand the special character of modern administration.

In modern society, according to Max Weber, it is the capitalist market economy which demands that bureaucratic tasks are accomplished as quickly as possible, as well as in a precise and singular manner.[88] The large capitalist enterprises are, according to Weber, usually exemplars of strict bureaucratic organization. Their business activities are focused on increasing precision, continuity and above all, on the operation proceeding quickly. According to Weber, this can only be achieved through strict bureaucratic organization. This bureaucratic organization develops technical dominance over all other forms of administration. Weber writes that a fully developed bureaucratic mechanism stands in the same relationship to all other administrative forms as a machine stands to non-mechanized production forms in the production of material goods.[89] Precision, speed, singularity, documentary knowledge, continuity, discretion, unity, strong discipline, lower levels of friction, lower transaction costs, fewer professional and personal strains, all these characteristics bring nearer the optimal, according to Weber, where the learned officer administers in a bureaucratic manner. In short, according to Weber, the modern bureaucracy is more rational than any other form of administration.

It is, therefore, Weber's thesis that the rationality which drives the capitalist production form installs itself in the modern bureaucracy of the state in the form of goal-oriented rational action. In this way, Weber believes that goal-oriented rational action not only comes to dominate in economic rationality, but also in the intervention of the state bureaucracy in social relations.

In Weber's theory, bureaucracy still has a limited importance with regard to social relations. In Weber's theory, civil society is still seen as an autonomous area in relation to the state bureaucracy. This opinion cannot be maintained in the modern welfare society. The modern welfare society is an administrative society in which the greater part of social life is touched by the state administration, and thereby also the rationality that is dominant within this administration. The dominance of goal-oriented rational action can in this way be strengthened in the social life of modern society.

In *Wirtschaft und Gesellschaft*, Weber summarized his view of modern society under the title "Legal Authority with a Bureaucratic Administrative Staff".[90] This summary falls into three sections, (1) the legitimacy of legal authority, (2) the fundamental categories of legal authority, and (3) legal authority as an ideal type, which is the bureaucratic administrative corps.

The Legitimacy of Legal Authority

According to Weber's theory, each administration is attached to a relation of authority. Weber sees his task as defining where in the relation of authority the modern bureaucracy lies. Weber differentiates between power and authority. He defines power as the ability to obtain one's will in a social context, even if this will meets resistance. A power relationship is characterized by there being no justification for the exercise of power. Authority from now on means the possibility of finding obedience for a command with a particular content from particular persons. All authority, according to Weber, requires some form of justification or legitimacy.[91] He who obeys a command must know why he obeys the command.

Weber divides up the different forms of authority based on the way they are legitimated. Here he operates with three forms of legitimate authority, namely, legal, traditional and charismatic. According to Weber, legal authority is associated with modern administration. Legal authority depends upon the belief in the legality of the given regime, and that those who are called upon to exercise authority do so based on the legal regime.[92] The validity or legitimacy of legal authority is based on the following five provisions:

1. The first provision is that through agreement or adoption, a law can be propagated which all members of the association (*Verband*) can follow.

In this definition, there exists an ambiguity in that the said law is made by agreement or adoption. Agreement implies that all members of the association reach consensus in making the law. This must mean a linguistically mediated agreement, as was described above in Habermas's theory of communicative action. By adoption, it is implied that the law is made without all members of the union having participated. The members who have not participated in the making of the law can rightly see this authority as being without legitimacy, that is, a relationship of power. In Weber's definition of legal authority, there is a lack of a clear distinction between authority and power.

2. Weber's second provision is that law forms an abstract totality of prudent rules which can be used in special cases, and that the bureaucracy takes care of the association's interests within the limits of the law.

This second provision builds upon the first. In so far as there was an ambiguity in the first provision, this ambiguity is carried over into the second provision. The talk about prudence is ambiguous. There can be different types of prudence, depending on whether the law was made through agreement or adoption. In the former case, what is prudent in the rules can be understood in relation to all members of the association. In the latter case, it cannot be expected that all members of the association see the law as an abstract totality of prudent rules. There is also an ambiguity in Weber's second provision about the relationship between authority and power.

3. Weber's third provision is that the person who exercises authority also must obey the impersonal regime which he in his ordinances refers to.

This ambiguity which arises in the first two provisions fades out in the third provision behind the assertion about the impersonal regime. The contradiction between agreement and adoption is covered over by the discussion of the impersonal regime. In this expression, it is no longer possible to maintain a distinction between power and authority. What is stated is that the administrator himself should obey the regime in which he finds himself when he gives commands and directives. But it remains unclear as to whether the impersonal regime, is an expression of authority or power. Therefore it remains unclear as to whether an administrator exercises power or authority. Whether or not it is power or authority on the order giving level, what remains is that on the receiving level, the administrator must obey incoming commands in the administrative regime. He may not erect a special regime for himself. In this sense it is possible to speak about an impersonal regime. In principle, personal standing is not taken into consideration.

4. Weber's fourth provision is that it is only as a member of the association that the member must uphold the law.

This provision states that the law is only applicable for the given association.

5. Weber's fifth provision is that a member's obedience is not based on the person who is invested with authority, but rather the impersonal regime, and therefore the member's obligation is only towards this rational delimited impartial regime.

This provision states that the member should not obey the administrator, but rather the impersonal regime which the administrator represents. But as Weber's theory is unclear as to whether the impersonal regime is an expression of authority or power, it remains unclear as to whether the member is obedient to power or authority.

In conclusion, there is an ambiguity in Weber's theory on the legitimacy of legal authority. It is not clear whether modern administration is an expression of legitimate authority or an exercise of power.

The Fundamental Categories of Legal Authority

Based on this conception of the legitimacy of legal authority, Weber formulated eight assertions or fundamental categories about the institutionalization of this authority in modern bureaucracy. The rationality of modern bureaucracy is expressed in these eight basic provisions:

1. Official tasks are organized in a continuously regulated manner.

What is stated here is that what is being discussed is an institution, in that an institution is precisely characterized by a continuous regulation of a social matter.

2. Official tasks are divided up into functionally different areas, each of which is equipped with the necessary authority and sanctions. The competence to act within such an area is called authority.

This means that administration must be divided into areas, such that the administrator's tasks can be handled in the most expedient way.

3. Offices are arranged hierarchically, and rights of control and complaint between them are specified.

This hierarchical organization is, according to Weber, most rational because it ensures that legal authority can be applied between administrative institutions. To this extent, hierarchy is rationally based. This comes to expression in that it is not just rights of control that are specified. It also includes the right to complain if the legal regulations are not upheld.

4. The rules which are followed can either be of a technical or normative character. In order to obtain the most rational course of action in both cases, a specialized education is required. Bureaucrats should have a specialized education.

What is said here is that a professional insight into the rules of administration is always required, regardless of whether the rules are of a technical or normative character.

5. The resources of the administration are sharply differentiated from the private resources of the administrative staff.

What Weber means here is that administration is an institution of legal authority which should not be combined with the administrator's private interests.

6. In an entirely rational administration, an office holder cannot treat his office as his property.

This point follows from the preceding in that it is not advantageous for the individual administrator to appropriate his office. In this case one cannot speak of legal authority, but rather corruption.

7. Administration is based on written documents, and this has a tendency to make the 'office' the centre of any modern bureaucracy.

Writing is at the centre of administration because it is writing that makes it possible to verify if legality is upheld.

8. Legal authority can take many different forms, but the most pure ideal typical form is found in the bureaucratic administrative corps.

Here, Weber means that the most rational administration is achieved when the individual administrator acts in rational accordance with the administrative institution, as outlined below.

By way of conclusion, it should be noted that the ambiguity of legal authority pointed out earlier is carried on in the fundamental categories of legal authority, and therefore also in the administrative institutions, at the same time that this ambiguity is veiled. In bureaucratic institutions, legal authority is administered; but it is nowhere stated in Weber's eight provisions as to whether legal authority is an expression of power or authority. The distinction between power and authority fades out in Weber's administrative institutions.

The Ideal Type of Legal Authority

After discussing legal authority's legitimacy and central categories in the bureaucratic institution, Weber proceeds to define legal authority in its most rational form, which is the bureaucratic administrative corps. In its most pure form, the administrative corps consists of what Weber calls "Einzelbeamten" which can be translated as the individual or independent officer or bureaucrat. The point is that it is the individual administrator who comprises the core of the ideal type, and the individual administrator who then should act out of the rationality which is laid down in the bureaucratic institution. Weber presents the following 10 provisions:

1. The members of the administrative corps are personally free and should only obey the duties of their office.
2. Officers are ordered in a set hierarchy.
3. Officers have clearly defined spheres of competence.
4. The appointment of officers is based on contracts.
5. Bureaucrats are selected based on their qualifications in the field, which in the most rational cases are ascertained on the basis of a test in the subject with a diploma.
6. Bureaucrats are paid with wages and are normally entitled to a pension. Wages are graduated based on one's position in the hierarchy. Bureaucrats can always resign their post, and in certain cases can be dismissed.
7. The bureaucratic post is his only or most important occupation.
8. A career structure exists and promotion is possible based either on seniority or competence or on the judgement of superiors.
9. The bureaucrat can appropriate neither his position, nor the resources which follow with it, as his own property.
10. The bureaucrat is part of a strict, coherent control and discipline system.

The essential point here is that the legal authority institutionalized in the administrative institution is carried out in relation to the administrator by 'doubling' the person in the role of administrator. The administrative corps' members are free, as indicated in Provision 1, and at the same time they are obliged to obey the duties of their office. This means that it is only in the role of the administrator that the person must obey the duties of the office. The person is only related to administration in so much as the person bears the role. But it also conversely implies that the person in the role of administrator must totally submit to the legal authority as it is mediated in the administrative institution. This is specified in Provisions 2, 3, 7 and 10. The administrator represents a professional knowledge (Provision 5) which is of essential importance for his placement in the bureaucratic hierarchy (Provisions 6 and 8).

Weber imagines that by doubling the person in the administrative role, it is possible to carry out legal authority in the administrative institution's hierarchical organization from top to bottom. In this conception the original ambiguity of legal authority is entirely suppressed: The individual administrator should act obediently towards his superiors, who on their part should follow the law, be this an adopted or a given law. The rationality in

Weber's theory is built upon the possibility of bridging legal authority and the actions of the individual administrator, and this bridge is sustained by the individual administrator's obedience in the hierarchical administrative institution.

Niklas Luhmann's System Oriented Administrative Theory

Weber's theory of modern bureaucracy has achieved such great importance because it emphasizes the rational character of administration. It is, however, precisely on this point of rationality that Weber's theory of administration has been criticized. Here we will look at Niklas Luhmann's system oriented critique of Weber's theory of bureaucracy.[93]

Luhmann's essential point is that rationality at the level of individual action is not the same as rationality at the social system level. In other words, the rationality of a social system cannot be secured solely by all individuals acting rationally.[94] What Luhmann means by system is an order of relations through which parts are tied together to form a whole, and the relationship between the whole and its parts is understood as a means-ends relation.[95] Luhmann wants to apply a system-theoretical, rather than an action-theoretical perspective to modern administration.

What is interesting here is that Luhmann reaches this new perspective by way of a critique of the central categories in Weber's theory. The focus here is on the means-ends model, the hierarchy of command and authority as a general means. The point here is that an understanding of the organization cannot lead back to these basic categories. On the contrary, they must be seen as variables, on the same level as a number of other variables in the empirical investigation of an organization understood as a system. All parts of the system should be seen as means towards the goal of the whole. The parts which do not allow themselves to be integrated into this optic are seen as interference of the system by its surrounding. The goal of a system is to maintain itself in relation to its surroundings and the outside world.[96]

It is in this context that Luhmann speaks of an autopoietic system. The idea of the autopoietic system is taken from biology, where the concept refers to a living system's ability to sustain itself. It is this thought that Luhmann imports into a social science context. Luhmann gives the following definition of an autopoietic system:

> As autopoeitic, we would call systems which themselves produce and reproduce the elements which they consist of, through the elements which they consist of. Everything which such systems use as a whole, be it their elements, their processes, their structures, and themselves are initially decided by precisely such units in the system. Or, put another way: There is neither an input of a unity in the system or output of a unity in the system. The system operates as a self-referential closed system. This does not mean that there are no relations with the outside world, it only means that these relations lie on another dimension of reality than the autopoies itself. It is often, with reference to Maturana, called a coupling of the system to its surroundings.[97]

The autopoietic system, according to Luhmann, maintains itself by independently producing and reproducing its own parts. Unity in the system is thus neither given beforehand in the form of an input, or as a result in the form of an output. The system sustains itself first and foremost through internal reference, that is to say, the system references itself. In this connection, Luhmann speaks of an autopoietic system as being self-referential. This is the meaning of the word 'autopoiesis'. Autopoiesis is related to the Greek word 'auto-poietikos' which means to make things oneself.

What is of interest now, is that it is through communication the social system maintains itself. Communication in this way becomes central in the autopoietic system.[98] What is brought in here is another conception of communication than that found in Habermas. Communication, according to Luhmann, is neither intentionally nor linguistically based, but based only in a consciousness of difference.[99] Communication is understood as an exchange of different perspectives on the same situation. This exchange is mediated through media and codes.[100] In this way, according to Luhmann, it is possible to create a continuous flow of information, which makes it possible to maintain a relatively stable system.[101]

Habermas's Critique of Luhmann's Theory of Administration

Habermas follows Luhmann in criticizing Weber's theory of administration. Modern administration, also according to Habermas, must be understood from a system-oriented perspective. But Habermas is also critical of looking exclusively at administration from this perspective. The problem for Habermas is that the administrative organization achieves its system-oriented autonomy by delimiting itself from the life world's symbolic structure. In this way, the organization achieves an indifference towards persons, society and culture.

This indifferent relationship between persons and organization is already present in Weber's theory, in so far as it was only the professional qualification and therefore professional people who were of interest. But at the same time, an ethic of calling was present in Weber's theory, according to which the individual almost becomes one with his position. This perspective is lost in Luhmann's system theory. Luhmann sees the person as an independent system, which forms an outside world for the administrative system. The person only partially enters into the administrative system in the form of the role of administrator. In this way the role of administrator comes to form a buffer-zone between the system and the person through which is it possible to create a distinction between the meaning context of systemic-oriented action and the personal meaning contexts and motivation structures which are rooted in the life world.[102] The role of administrator represents an internal system action which entirely conforms to the system-functional demands. In this optic, the person cannot manifest himself in relation to the role. The person is irrelevant to the system. The role adapts to the needs of the system. Any connection to the normative life world is seen as an externality by the administrative system.

Habermas sees a similar problem in Luhmann's theory on the relation between the administrative organization and society and culture. In Luhmann's theory, the administrative organization extricates itself from the established cultural traditions in order to create autonomous space for movement. This means that the organization itself has to cover its legitimacy needs. In this system-oriented perspective, law comes to replace the life world as the entity which legitimates system-oriented action.

In this context, according to Habermas, communicative action loses its validity foundation. The administrator acts communicatively under restraints.[103] The administrator knows that he can, not just in special circumstances, but at any time, depart from communicative action and retreat to the formal legal rules which form the basis of his role. In this way, language is separated from its interpersonal bindings. The ultimate reference of language is not to the life world, but rather to the legally formalized relations of the system. In this context, language does not necessarily serve communicative action; it creates legally formalized room for strategic action on the part of the administrator.

In conclusion, it can be said that Luhmann's system functionalism builds upon the precondition that bureaucracy has thoroughly infiltrated society, resulting in communicative action, with its rooting in the life world having already lost its decisive meaning in social life. On this point, Habermas proposes that modern society is split between life world and system world and that the system world is threatening to colonize the life world. Habermas, in agreement with Luhmann, believes that a system perspective must be applied to bureaucracy. The question is whether there should be an internal limit for this perspective. This will be considered in Chapter 3, where the role of the administrator is analyzed. First, we will look more closely at what system-oriented demands are made on the administrator. Subsequently, we will look at how these system demands can place the administrator in an ethical conflict which can only be resolved by personally taking a stand.

3 The Modern Administrator

The Administrator: Between Role and Person

As mentioned, this chapter analyzes the modern administrator. I define the administrator rather broadly as a social role within an administration which is carried out by a person. This definition coalesces with Weber's theory of the modern administrator. As we have just seen, Weber draws a sharp distinction between the person and the role. The individual must, so to speak, 'shed' the person when taking on the role. It is therefore the role which stands central in this theory. The same idea is found in Luhmann's theory. But there is the difference in that Luhmann does not conceive the administrator as becoming as much a part of his role as Weber does. In Luhmann's theory, the person comprises an independent system which only partially is included as a role in the administrative system. In Habermas's theory, the administrator is at one and the same time role and person. In the role, the administrator references the administrative system while, as a person, the administrator references civil society and the life world. Habermas's understanding of the administrator is the most extensive of the theories introduced here, because he includes the duality of the administrator *within* the administrative institution, while the other two theories in their own way exclude the person *from* the administrative institution. All three theories view the administrator as primarily a role within an administration. It is within this understanding that the following analysis proceeds. According to all three theories, the administrator acts in a goal-oriented rational manner within the administration. The administrator is constantly occupied with obtaining specific goals by employing appropriate means. The administrator therefore must continuously evaluate how he can act most prudently in relation to means and ends. Under closer scrutiny, this evaluation shows itself to be very complicated because neither means nor ends appear in unambiguous clarity. The administrator can be pressed by different referents, each of which places demands on the administrator which must at least be taken into consideration.[104] These referential entities can be divided into four ideal types. These are the administrator's relation to: the law, his superiors, his profession and civil society. Each of these referential entities place their own independent demands on the administrator, which may very well be in conflict with each other. In this way, the administrator can enter into a dilemma in which he personally must take a position on how he will act. Such position-taking demands normative evaluations of an ethical character to be made. In the following discussion, I will examine this issue in more detail, first on the ideal typical level by analyzing the four above named referents. Then I will present the ethical conflicts of the administrator.

The Administrator's Relationship to Law

First I will look at the administrator's relationship to law. Law is important for the administrator in many ways. One is that, like all other citizens, the administrator must heed the law. Law in this context has to do with obedience for the administrator. The other important aspect of law is that it forms the reference point for the administrator's goal-oriented rational action. Law in this case can be called the action referent of the administrator.

Earlier, I accounted for Weber's view of modern administration. It is Weber's belief that modern administration can be characterized as legal authority with a bureaucratic administrative staff. Implicit in legal authority is the idea that law is established through agreement or adopted through generally acknowledged (accepted) procedures, and that law then becomes the highest referent for the social order in society. Legal authority is then implemented or realized, according to Weber, most rationally through a bureaucratic administrative staff.

As noted earlier, it is difficult to draw a sharp boundary between authority and power in Weber's theory. The theory is laden with an issue of legitimacy. This has importance for the individual citizen, who justly can question the validity of a law and thereby the legitimacy of legal authority. In the same way, the issue of legitimacy is of importance for the individual administrator. He can in the same way question the validity of the existing administrative law.

In democratic society, law is legitimated through the democratic procedures. Law is applicable in so far as it is adopted through democratic procedures. This, however, does not mean that the law is legitimate. This is because the material law cannot be reduced to its relationship to the democratic procedure. Law has a substantial content which must be taken into account, and which easily can go against the individual citizen or the individual administrator's ideas of how the law *ought* to be formulated. The democratic procedure is not sufficient in itself for the individual citizen or administrator to legitimate the substantive content of a specific law. The substantive content of a particular law may be reprehensible, even though it is adopted through democratic procedures. In this case, it may appear obvious that the administrator does not want to uphold the law. But he must nevertheless. The question here is what can lie in this order. The problem is that the order cannot be accepted by free choice. But the order is put to the administrator anyway. This is done through power. This gives rise to a personal dilemma, which in its broadest consequence can become a matter of the extent to which the administrator is willing to maintain his resistance to the law and incur an eventual penalty. Law can, in other words, be the cause of an ethical dilemma for the administrator. The administrator can be brought into an ethical dilemma in relation to a particular law if he views this law as reprehensible. This is a dilemma which is not in principle different from the dilemmas other citizens face due to their general obligation to obey the law. The dilemma can, however, be more acute for the administrator because he has a much stricter relationship to the law than the general citizen.

The special importance of the law derives from the fact that the administrator acts in direct relation to the law. The law is the direct reference point for the administrator. According to Weber, this is because the law has come to play a similar role to that which the Protestant ethic played earlier in the institutionalization of goal-oriented rational action in modern society. As the Protestant ethic loses its direct importance as the basis for an ethic of calling, which according to Weber was essential in the constituting of the capitalist economy and administration, law comes in to take the place of ethics as the stabilizing guarantor for goal-oriented rational action in economics and administration. As noted in the above treatment of Weber's legal theory, the problem is that law has no ultimate normative meaning for the administrator. On the contrary, the rationalization of law, as seen above, leads to all normativity, understood as rational agreement, disappearing from law.

The function of law as a stabilizing guarantor of goal-oriented rational action is important for the administrator's discourse. When the administrator justifies his action, he does not need to act communicatively or illocutively. He can continuously step back from communicative action and act perlocutively in his discourse. He can continuously refer to the law as the highest level of appeal in communication. As stated in Chapter 1, perlocutive discourse is characterized by having its final references outside communication. The administrator can in this way act communicatively *with reservations*. The reservation consists of the possibility suspending communication at any time.

This is compounded by the fact that law is very seldom unambiguous. Law, as a rule, must be interpreted. The administrator then has the opportunity to interpret the law in a way which best serves his ends if he so desires. In this way, the law becomes an instrument in the administrator's goal-oriented rational action. The administrator is served by the law. That power, which in the first instance was exercised over the administrator, is then turned into a power at the disposal of the administrator. The administrator comes to exercise power through his action. In this context I define power as the opportunity to communicate *with reservations*.

The Administrator's Relation to Superiors

In the previous chapter we reviewed the different understandings of what it is that characterizes modern administration. That which was common to all understandings was the precondition that the administrator act in obedience to his superiors. Administration is organized hierarchically, in which each administrator stands in a relationship of obedience towards his superiors. This should not be read as meaning that the administrator continuously acts under orders. Most administrators have autonomous room for manoeuvring within which they can take independent decisions. The relation to the superior should be understood such that the administrator can ultimately refer to his superior who draws the overarching frame for the administrator. This is of importance for the administrator's relationship to his superiors.

The discourse of the administrator towards his superiors can be characterized in two ways. One can either speak of an explicit or an implicit reference. The administrator's discourse can, as mentioned above, be a perlocutive discourse. What is characteristic of perlocutive discourse is that it is ruled by external referents. In this case, the administrator's superior can implicitly or explicitly be this external referent for the administrator's discourse. In the first case, it is a matter of the administrator's discourse being directly decided by the superior's order or suggestion. The administrator is to do what the superior says. The superior can also be an implicit referent. In this case, the administrator can act based on what is expected of him. The administrator may interpret the wishes of his superior without them being explicitly expressed. In this case, the superior has a hidden position in the administrator's perlocutive discourse. In summary, the superior is always present in the administrator's perlocutive discourse as the ultimate referent. It is this presence which maintains the perlocutive character in the administrator's discourse.

In the review of the administrator's relationship to law, it was highlighted that the administrator uses law as an instrument in his perlocutionary discourse. Law served as a substitute reference for communication. In the administrator's relationship to his superiors, the situation is different. It is merely the presence of the superior which forces speech's conversion from illocution to perlocution. The superior is ever present as an ultimate reference, which is decisive for the administrator's discourse. This could also be understood as the administrator being forced to abandon illocutionary communication. The administrator is forced into perlocutionary discourse.

The Administrator's Relationship to his Profession

Weber defines the administrator as a professional person who has been through a professional education which preferably has culminated in an acknowledged diploma. The profession is an important reference for the administrator. The administrator's professional reference is of a different character than the two other references outlined above. The reference to profession has a relatively autonomous relationship to the administration and does not directly allow itself to be subordinated to law or ends which are set by the administration's leadership. This is because the professional reference represents an independent form of understanding which is rooted in some institutional and systematic contexts which do not necessarily have a connection to the administration. For example, when a biologist is employed by the Ministry of Fisheries to give an overview of the ecological situation in the seas around Denmark, his rooting in biology as a discipline will give him an independent reference which has no connection to the administration in the Ministry of Fisheries. The same would be the case for a profession such as law, which otherwise has been closely associated with administration. There is no profession that does not have its own professional discourse.

The special professional discourse has an autonomy which must be seen in connection with the professional discourse's basis in the scientific institution. This rooting gives the professional discourse a communicative character, in as much as all science basically must build upon an equal and free discussion among the implicated partners.

In administration, however, professional discourse is brought into an instrumental or strategic connection. Discourse is not conducted for its own sake, it is conducted for a reason which is decided outside the discourse. Or, possibly more correctly, pressure on the professional discourse is exercised by the superiors and from the side of institutional reproduction in general. In as much as the administrator himself is an active actor in the administration, he also introduces the professional discourse into a strategic context in the form of perlocutionary discourse. In this way professional discourse is turned into technocratic discourse.

Technocratic discourse is characterized by the professional discourse being expropriated from its professional and social context and is subordinated to the administration's goal-oriented rational action. In this way professional discourse is shielded from the internal reflection which characterizes scientific discourse. Professional discourse is determined by an external goal set by the administration.

The Administrator's Relation to Civil Society

The administrator's relation to civil society is the last reference to be analyzed. This reference is complicated because it contains an ambiguity. The administrator on the one hand as a person is a citizen in civil society, and on the other hand in the role of administrator stands over civil society. As a person, the administrator is rooted in civil society. In this respect he shares the same experiential reference points as everyone else in society. As a person he is enmeshed in the communicative discourses of civil society.

On the other hand, in the role of administrator, the aspect of person is often shed, at least partially. The administrator acts on behalf of the administration with regard to civil society. What takes place in this context is goal-oriented rational action which is characterized by perlocutionary discourse.

It is in the administrator's relation to civil society that this split becomes most evident. On the one hand the administrator conducts a perlocutive discourse with the members of civil society, and in this meaning instrumentalizes his relationship to the citizen. On the other hand, the administrator as a person is enmeshed in the same social context he instrumentalizes.

Demands on the Administrator

The investigation so far has shown that the administrator finds himself in a force field drawn by four poles. These four poles place different demands on the administrator, all of which should be integrated into his goal-oriented rational action. In the following discussion I will look at how the administrator condenses the demands from these four poles or entities into one goal-oriented rational action, and how this comes to expression in the administrator's discourse.

The administrator has to try condense the demands from the different entities in one coherent action, which comes to expression in one coherent discourse. This discourse is of a perlocutory character, in so far as it is determined by entities outside the discourse. The administrator may be able to argue rationally for his actions taking into consideration the external referents. The principal issue for the administrator is how he can condense or summarize the demands from the different referents. In this context one can differentiate between two different situations for the administrator. In the first case, compatible demands are made on the administrator. By this I mean demands which can be united or reconciled. In the second case, contradictory demands are made. By this I mean demands which cannot be united or reconciled.

In the first case, where compatible demands are made on the administrator that can be accomplished simultaneously, the administrator can reconcile the demands based on a criterion of prudence. What is prudent can be governed purely by the internal relation to the referents which make demands on the administrator. The administrator can attempt to obtain the optimal in relation to the demands from the different entities.

Situations can arise where contradictory demands are placed on the administrator. In this case, the contradictory demands cannot be reconciled in perlocutionary discourse. Perlocutionary discourse is characterized by the fact that it refers to external referents. But in this case, where the external referents are in conflict, and where they manifest themselves with comparable strength, the administrator can no longer directly strike a compromise between the different referents in his discourse. This means that the administrator can no longer make a choice *within* the framework of the role of administrator. He is forced to independently or personally make a decision as to how he will act, and he alone may bear the consequences of his actions. In this way, the administrator is brought into an ethical conflict.

The Administrator's Ethical Dilemma

In the beginning of this chapter, the administrator was defined as a role which is borne by a person. The point in this definition is that the administrator functions as a role within an administration understood as a social system. A role cannot support itself, it has to be borne by a person. The person, from this perspective, becomes a type of unavoidable appendage to the role. From a system perspective, it is the role that is central and important.

The problem now is that the role can only remain when compatible demands are made on it. In the case where contradictory demands are made, it can no longer be remain so. Contradictory demands are those which cannot be accomplished at the same time and are mutually exclusive. In this way, the contradictory demand is shifted from the role of administrator to the person who bears the administrator's role. The person himself has to decide how he will act. The person is thereby put in an ethical dilemma. An ethical dilemma is defined as a situation where the given references for action have lost their direct relevance and where it becomes an open question for the person to decide how he will act.[105] In this context, two forms of conflict can be discerned. There can be a situation of an ethical dilemma arising in relation to a single referent, or a dilemma arising from the relation between different referents. In this context, it is possible to construct ideal types of these two forms of conflict. I will first take up the ethical dilemma arising from a single referent.

The law forms the normative system which the administrator is obliged to obey. As I have already noted a number of times, law is infused with an ambiguity in that for the individual person it is not entirely clear whether law is accepted or given. There is then a problem of acknowledgement in relation to law, which leads to the question of whether the administrator should obey the law. Seen from Weber's perspective, the administrator should always uphold the law. The same is true from Luhmann's system-theoretical perspective. In both theories, the administrator is viewed as a role. The problem, however, is that the role is borne by a person who, in the final instance, bears responsibility in relation to the law. This view accords with Habermas's theory. It is the person who is held responsible if the administrator does not follow the law. It is, therefore, the person who in the final instance is left with the problem of acknowledging the law and taking responsibility for acting in accordance with it. But this is not necessarily possible for the person. As mentioned earlier, demands from the law can be made on the person which he cannot accept. In this case, the administrator is dragged into a personal conflict. It is in the role of administrator that he meets the law, but as a person that he must make decisions with regard to it. There is then a shift in relation to law from the role of administrator to the administrator's person.

A similar situation can arise between the administrator and his superiors. According to the way the administration is structured, the administrator must obey his superiors. But should he do this under all conditions? According to Weber, the administrator should obey his superiors as long as his superiors give orders within the law. But even in this case, a superior can give an order which the administrator finds wrong to obey. In this case there is also a shifting of the conflict from the role to the person. It is in his role that the administrator must obey his superiors, but it is as a person that he bears responsibility for his actions.

According to Weber, the administrator is a professional. It is on the basis of his professional education that the administrator joins the administration. All professions have their normative codes. By this I mean the norms about how the profession is carried out in the proper way. A number of conflicts can also arise between the profession and its integration in the administration. In such cases it is also the person who must decide whether his profession is carried out properly in the administration.

The administrator plays a role in his relation to citizens and civil society. But he personally is responsible for his action. Conflicts can also arise here between the administrator's action in his role as administrator and his personal belief about that action. It is only as a person that the administrator can take a position on such actions.

It is not only in relation to single referents that ethical dilemmas can arise for the administrator. Ethical dilemmas can equally arise due to the relationship between different referents. The administrator is presented with normative demands from the four referents, each demanding to be met. It is then up to the administrator to amalgamate these different demands into one discourse and one action. But the demands can very easily be of a contradictory character, because they originate from four different value spheres or domains which initially have nothing to do with each other. In such cases, the administrator must again take a personal position on how to act and bear responsibility for this action.

To summarize, the administrator can be subjected to a demand from the different individual referents which he finds it wrong to carry out, or he can be subjected to demands from the different referents which require contradictory actions. In both cases, the administrator is presented with demands which he cannot fulfill within his role, and he must then make a personal decision and personally take responsibility for his actions. In other words, the conflict is shifted from the role to the person who bears the role. The problem here is how the person is to find a referent upon which to base his decision, as he can no longer employ the referents which form the foundation of his role. It is this issue which is taken up in the following chapter on the relationship between ethics and administration.

4 Ethics and Administration

In the following chapter, the problem of ethics confronting the administrator will be more closely investigated. Ethics is a philosophical discipline which has its origins in Greek philosophy. It is first and foremost Aristotle who gave the discipline a name. Ethics comes from the Greek word *ethos* which means custom. Custom in this context refers broadly to the customary norms in a society which are implemented or realized without questioning. Ethics deals with considerations of situations where custom has lost its direct relevance or validity, and where how to act becomes an open question. Ethics thus deals with the reflective relationship of the setting of norms.

By extension, a differentiation can be made between ethics and morality. Moral comes from the Latin word *mores* which also means custom and practice. The term moral is generally used to express given or customary normative references which have not lost their direct relevance or validity. In summary, one can say that ethics consciously sets norms, while with morality, norms are given.

Ethics has traditionally dealt with the personal setting of norms. In ethics, it is traditionally the person who is at the centre. This understanding has become too restrictive in modern society. This is because it is not only persons who come into situations of conflict where the customary normative references have lost their direct relevance. This is also the case for people in social roles. This, for example, is the case with administrators. It is therefore obvious to rework the concept of ethics so that it also applies to persons who act in social roles. Such an undertaking is not, however, unproblematic, because a role cannot be held accountable for actions. Only a person can. As long as ethics also deals with responsibility for the choice of norms which form the basis for action, one can only really speak in this context of ethics in relation to a person. But in so much as the person bears responsibility for his role, one can also speak of ethics in relation to the social role, in the sense that ethical dilemmas can arise for the person in the social role for which the person ultimately must bear responsibility. With such a distinction, one can speak of a hierarchy of different forms of ethics.

Ethics can be discussed on the level of the social role, but this form of ethics has a defined boundary which points back at the person, and thereby to personal ethics. By extension of this logic, one can speak of role ethics and personal ethics. In our case the role ethic deals with the administrator's role, so we can differentiate between administrative ethics and personal ethics. In the following pages we will look closer at both of these forms of ethics.

Weber's Administrative Ethics

The Protestant Ethic of Calling

Differentiating between personal and role ethics has, as previously mentioned, a long tradition in Protestant theology, where Luther introduced a distinction between the spiritual and the worldly regimes. In the spiritual realm, the person should obey God, and in the worldly regime, the person in his calling and estate should obey the worldly rulers.

Weber builds upon this tradition. In *The Protestant Ethic and the Spirit of Capitalism*, Weber shows how Protestantism leads to the establishment of a special ethic of calling, which I have already reviewed. The ethic of calling is built on the dichotomy between the spiritual and the worldly which Luther formulated. From a sociological perspective, this can be understood as a freeing of the worldly. In other words, Protestantism set secularization in motion. In this, the worldly is seen as an independent sphere of action. Each individual should act in his calling and estate obediently towards his superiors, who are also called authorities. Authorities, according to Luther, are installed by God to uphold the bourgeois order with the help of the sword. Weber then shows, as noted above in *The Protestant Ethic and the Spirit of Capitalism,* that the religious foundation for the ethic of calling dissolves by itself, in the course of the worldly domain coming to stand on its own feet, without reference to the spiritual domain. This secularization process is driven forward by the capitalist oriented bourgeoisie's drive to accumulate money and capital. In this way, goal-oriented rational action, as shown earlier, becomes the dominant social rationality. What is paradoxical, however, is that in spite of Weber making note of the fact that the religious foundation for the ethic of calling is dissolved through the secularization process into pure goal-oriented rational action, it is precisely the calling idea from the Protestant tradition which he carries over into his definition and discussion of a special administrative ethic.

Weber's Administrative Ethics

In his lecture, *Politik als Beruf* Weber describes the administrator's special ethical situation in the following way:

> ... the genuine official...will not engage in politics. Rather, he should engage in impartial 'administration'. (...) *Sine ira et studio* 'without scorn and bias' he shall administer his office. Hence, he shall *not* do precisely what the politician, the leader as well as his following, must always and necessarily do, namely, *fight*. To take a stand, to be passionate – *ira et studium* – is the politician's element, and above all the element of the political *leader*. His conduct is subject to quite a different, indeed, exactly the opposite, *principle of responsibility* from that of the civil servant. The honor of the civil servant is vested in his ability to execute conscientiously the order of the superior authorities, exactly as if the order agreed with his own convictions. (...) Without this moral discipline and self-denial, in the highest sense, the whole apparatus would fall to pieces. The honor of the political leader, of the leading statesmen, however, lies precisely in an exclusive *personal* responsibility for what he does, a responsibility he cannot and must not reject or transfer.[106]

The main issue in Weber's lecture is politics as a life calling. In this connection, Weber presents very powerfully the politician's ethical situation in relation to the administrator's ethical situation, and thereby touches on the administrator's ethical situation. Briefly, Weber's position is that the politician should fight for his opinions and take responsibility for his actions. The administrator should be obedient towards his superiors. This leads to the administrator's special dilemma; namely that he should, in spite of his personal convictions, carry out orders just as conscientiously as if the orders were in accordance with his own personal convictions. One can say that the administrator's ethical dilemma is shifted to another level, in that the administrator must account for when he will give up his own personal convictions and carry out the given order. The administrator is thus answerable for his own actions, even though he carries out the will of another. This creates a highly complicated ethical situation for the administrator.

This situation is not made less complicated by the fact that the administrator, as stated above, not only acts in reference to his superiors, but also to a number of other referents, such as the law, his profession, citizens and civil society. The administrator also, under normal conditions, stands in a situation in which he as administrator must make independent decisions which imply responsibility and thereby an ethical dimension. This situation can be even more complicated if the administrator is subjected to contradictory demands from the four referents, and thereby must personally take a stand on what the right course of action should be. In practice, a sharp distinction cannot be maintained between the ethical situations of the politician and the administrator, as Weber presents. The administrator must also bear responsibility for his actions. This leads to consideration of the ethical considerations upon which the administrator should base his actions. In this connection, it can be useful to bring in Weber's discussion of 'ethics of ultimate ends' and ethics of responsibility.

Weber's Ethic of Responsibility

Weber's Ethic of Ultimate Ends and Ethics of Responsibility

Weber introduces a distinction between ethics of ultimate ends and ethics of responsibility in his lecture *Politik als Beruf*, where he writes:

> We must be clear about the fact that all ethically oriented conduct may be guided by one of two fundamentally differing and irreconcilably opposed maxims: conduct can be oriented to an 'ethic of ultimate ends' or to an 'ethic of responsibility'. This is not to say that an ethic of ultimate ends is identical with irresponsibility, or that an ethic of ultimate ends is identical with unprincipled opportunism. Naturally nobody says that. However, there is an abysmal contrast between conduct that follows the maxim of an ethic of ultimate ends – that is, in religious terms, 'The Christian does rightly and leaves the results with the Lord' – and conduct that follows the maxim of an ethic of responsibility, in which case one has to give an account of the foreseeable results of one's action.
>
> You may demonstrate to a convinced syndicalist, believing in an ethic of ultimate ends, that his action will result in increasing the opportunities of

> reaction, in increasing the oppression of his class, and obstructing its ascent – and you will not make the slightest impression upon him. If an action of good intent leads to bad results, then, in the actor's eyes, not he but the world, or the stupidity of other men, or God's will who made them thus, is responsible for the evil. However a man who believes in an ethic of responsibility takes account of precisely the average deficiencies of people; as Fichte has correctly said, he does not even have the right to presuppose their goodness and perfection. He does not feel in a position to burden others with the results of his own actions so far as he was able to foresee them; he will say: these results are ascribed to my action.[107]

Weber presents two forms of ethics, based on whether the action is good in itself, or whether the consequences of the action are good.

The first form of ethics, ethics of ultimate ends, is the unconditional form of ethics which has its roots in the Judeo-Christian religious tradition and in modern times was reformulated by Kant in philosophical terms. The unconditionality in this ethics revolves precisely around it examining the actions themselves, independent of the consequences of the action. In the religious language of the Judeo-Christian tradition, an unconditional demand about how one should act is made. In the Old Testament, it is formulated as God's unconditional law, better known as the Ten Commandments. In the New Testament, it is formulated as the unconditional demand to love one's neighbor. Kant reformulated the content of this tradition with reason as the supreme arbiter. The whole of Kant's ethical project set out to create an ethic independent of arbitrary historical circumstances, human inclinations, impulses, etc. Kant summarized his ethic in the following formulation: You should act in such as way that the maxim of your action can become a law for the action of others.

It is in contrast to the ethics of conscience that Weber sets up his ethics of responsibility. Weber's ethics of responsibility is a form of consequentialist ethics. In the ethic of responsibility, the action is not judged in itself, but rather in relation to the consequences of the action. Here Weber writes:

> No ethics in the world can dodge the fact that in numerous instances the attainment of the 'good' ends is bound to the fact that one must be willing to pay the price of using morally dubious means, or at least dangerous ones, and facing the possibility, or even the probability of evil ramifications. From no

> ethics in the world can it be concluded when and to what extent the ethically good purpose 'justifies' the ethically dangerous means and ramifications.[108]

Weber's ethic of responsibility has great similarities to utilitarianism in that both are goal or consequence-oriented ethics.

Utilitarianism

Utilitarianism is the label applied to a wide tradition of ethics established by Bentham in the beginning of the 1800s. According to utilitarianism, the ethically correct action is that which compared with other possible actions, brings the greatest number of positive values. That is to say, the value of an action is dependent on its ability to bring about the greatest number of positive values of a non-ethical nature, be it happiness, wealth, good health, beauty, insight, etc. This definition closely approximates Weber's definition of goal-oriented rational action. According to Weber, goal-oriented rational action is all about finding the best means to obtain a particular result, considering the side effects of different possible actions. One could with good reason say that utilitarianism is the ethical theory which corresponds to goal-oriented rational action. This is the reason why utilitarianism is so wide spread in our society. It coalesces well with the dominance of goal-oriented rational action.

Utilitarianism possesses the same strengths and weaknesses as goal-oriented rational action. The strength of utilitarianism lies in it being a formal ethical theory which deals exclusively with relative values. This makes it an operational or calculable ethical theory. Both means and ends can be calculated. The slogan of utilitarianism could be 'the greatest good for the greatest number', while at the same time harming as few as possible. It is exactly this consideration which can be said to be the ethical theory of goal-oriented rational action. When one, for example, calculates the balance between speed limits and traffic fatalities, it is precisely such calculations which are made. On the one hand, there is an interest in having as high a speed limit as possible. On the other hand, there is an interest in having as few people as possible die in traffic accidents.

Now we have arrived at the difficulties with utilitarian ethics. Based on this ethical theory, it is impossible to derive how utility is established. Utilitarianism is based on the idea that norms or utility are pre-given, or possesses an obvious clarity, so that it is not necessary to establish what utility substantively consists of.

The other difficulty in utilitarianism is that it is not possible for it to resolve the problem that by obtaining the greatest good for the greatest number, there are almost always some people who are excluded from drawing benefit from the activity. The theory then contains the possibility of passing over a victim in silence.

Utilitarianism has limitations, in that the theory raises ethical problems that cannot be answered within the theory itself.

The Administrator and Utilitarianism

Utilitarianism could be called the administrator's ethics, in so far as the administrator acts with goal-oriented rationality within the administration. The administrator is faced with making a decision based upon demands and goals which are set by the four referents presented above. As long as the administrator is presented only with compatible demands, that is to say demands which are reconcilable, utilitarianism raises no problems for him. On the contrary, it is wholly within the administration's operational logic that the administrator tries to find the best means to achieve the goal which he is presented with. But as soon as the administrator is presented with contradictory demands from the different referents which must be taken into consideration before acting, the goal of the administrator's action is no longer unambiguously clear. Here a problem arises for the administrator, as it is impossible for utilitarianism to justify the validity of a norm. This could be called the limitation of administrator's ethic, in so far as the conflict cannot be solved within the framework of administrative ethics. The conflict is then transferred from the administrator to the person in the administrative role. The person then must decide how he will act as an administrator. This raises new ethical problems which fall under the category of personal ethics.

Weber's Ethic of Responsibility in Relation to Utilitarianism.

As mentioned above, Weber's ethic of responsibility has great similarities to utilitarianism, in that both are goal or consequence-oriented ethics. Weber's ethic of responsibility is not a pure form of utilitarianism, in the sense that moral consideration of means must be undertaken. Weber can speak of morally considered means. For Weber, however, it is beyond the scope of ethical consideration to evaluate means in relation to goals, and equally it lies beyond the scope of this ethics to evaluate ends or goals. The ethical choice, according to Weber, is ultimately conditional or contingent.

Weber is correct in stating that pure ethics of conscience has some serious weaknesses. It is true that an action cannot be evaluated on its own, it must be evaluated in its context. But Weber's ethic does not solve these problems because this ethic gives no indication of how we should evaluate the validity of an action. It is this issue which the German philosopher Karl-Otto Apel takes up in his criticism of Weber's ethic of responsibility.

There is a close connection between Apel and Habermas, in that under mutual inspiration, they have formulated different versions of the special form of ethics called discursive ethics or communicative ethics. When I, in this case choose to focus more on Apel than Habermas, it is because Apel has dealt more extensively with Weber's ethic of responsibility than Habermas, and Apel has also tried to formulate his own ethic of responsibility, which Habermas has not.

Apel's Ethic of Responsibility

Apel's Critique of Weber's Ethic of Responsibility

In his article *Konfliktlösung im Atomzeitalter als Problem einer Verantwortungsethik*, Apel bases his attempt to formulate an ethic of responsibility on a critique of Weber's ethic of responsibility. According to Apel, the problem with Weber's ethic of responsibility is that ultimately, it is not possible for Weber to give a rational justification for ethics.[109] Ethics to Weber, according to Apel, is exclusively a matter for a 'private decision based on belief'.[110] According to Weber, the only thing that can be rationally justified is the value free consideration of possible consequences of an action.[111] Weber, according to Apel, is only concerned with the issue of goal-oriented rational action. The reason why Apel remains interested in Weber from a philosophical perspective is because according to Apel, Weber acknowledges that goal-oriented rational action raises ethical issues which Weber doesn't believe can be solved rationally. Fundamental ethical choice, according to Weber, is irrational. To summarize Apel's position, he believes Weber raises the right issues in relation to the validity of ethics of responsibility, but gives the wrong solution.

Apel's Discursive Ethics

In his attempt to solve the problem of giving the ethic of responsibility a foundational basis, Apel takes as his point of departure the differentiation between the various types of rationality presented in Chapter 1. Apel's primary criticism of Weber is that he has too restricted an understanding of rationality, in that he is only oriented towards goal-oriented rationality, and especially strategic rationality. Apel, in concurrence with Habermas, introduces communicative rationality as the foundation for the establishment of ethical norms. Apel writes:

> Should this purely strategic orientation be prevented by a morality of ultimate ends – which is Kant's position – then the continuously acknowledged norm of rationality must be an *a priori* acknowledged *non purely strategic rationality*: that is to say, as a norm for legeslative rationality, which in advance generalizes a non-strategic, mutuality between people, which, in a Kantian context, not only acknowledges the other as a *means* to the realization of one's own interests, but always also as *a being which is an end in itself*, in the meaning of a 'kingdom of ends'. But how can it be rationally compellingly demonstrated, that we have already acknowledged such a fundamental norm for rationality, and not just a strategic rationality.[112]

Apel raises the question of how a pure strategic orientation can be limited by a moral orientation. If this is possible, it must be possible to postulate a form of reason which is non-strategic in character, according to which the other is not just a strategic means, but rather a goal in itself. The problem is whether or not one can argue convincingly for such a form of reason. Apel advances the following argumentation:

> I also believe that it is possible to demonstrate this after one has made the following clear: *The intersubjectively valid argumentative rationality of thought* cannot, in principle, be a matter of the individual thinking subject's strategic instrumental rationality; it must rather in principle require the possibility for reaching concensus between equal members of an unlimited discursive community. To admit this requires overcoming the traditional conception that the individual alone, based on his cognitive functioning, that is

> to say without the stipulation of linguistic meaning which he can share with others, can *think* and *acknowledge*. But if one admits this, one can also admit that anyone who thinks in accord with the validity principle, that is to say, argues, has also already implicitly acknowledged the normative obligations of the ethic of the ideal communicative community. This means that, he has necessarily, among other things, implicitly accepted the following: Conflicts between people should not be resolved by violence or threats of violence, not even through strategic negotiations which lead to the suppression of legitimate interests.
>
> Such an ethical *foundational norm for the discursive reaching of consensus* is even automatically followed by he who posits the opposite, for in so far as he *argues seriously*, he demonstrates that this foundational norm cannot be objected to without *engaging in self-contradictory behavior*. And this is perfectly sufficient for an ultimate philosophical justification. This means that it *does not need to be derived from anything else*, neither *inductively* nor *deductively*.[113]

Apel asserts that argumentative reason necessarily differs radically from the individual thinking subject's strategic goal-oriented rationality. Argumentative, or communicative reason must be built upon the principle that it is possible to reach agreement among equal partners in a boundary-less argumentation community or communicative community. In this conception, Apel breaks with the traditional concept of reason, according to which reason is associated with the isolated individual subject's consciousness, independent of the linguistic meanings which must be shared with others. Furthermore, Apel contends that communicative reason is bound up with the linguistic community between people, and that it is totally impossible to think and recognize things independent of this linguistic community. This is equivalent to Habermas's view as presented in Chapter 1. The consequence of this assumption, according to Apel, is that everyone who thinks using a criterion of validity, that is to say, argues, already has acknowledged the normative obligation of an ethic for the ideal communicative community. Intrinsic in such an ethic must be the idea that conflicts should not be solved by power or the threat of power, not even through strategic action, which can lead to the subjugation of legitimate interests. Rather, conflicts ought to be solved through reasoned discourse in which all implicated legitimate interests are exposed in the discussion, so that a decision can be taken which all interested parties can agree upon.

Apel's decisive argument for the foundational norm of this discursive consensus is that even the person who proposes the opposite follows this norm, in so far as he argues sincerely for his position. The norm then cannot be contested without what Apel calls 'pragmatic contradictions' arising. The point here is that the ethic is founded in the very way in which language operates. Language is fundamentally characterized by mutuality, and one cannot sincerely argue against this mutuality through language without a contradiction arising between the expression and the content of expression. The expression itself comes to confirm the mutuality, despite the fact that the content of the expression may be aimed at contesting this mutuality. Apel calls this argumentation discourse ethics' transcendental pragmatic *Letzbegründung*, that is to say, discourse ethics' final and decisive justification. According to Apel, this does not need to be derived from anything else, be it inductive or deductive.

Apel's Ethic of Responsibility

Apel's formulation of discourse ethics represents an abstract ethic of conscience like that of Kant. Fundamentally it is a Kantian ethic, in which the final referent is moved from reason, as in Kant, to a reason which is communicatively founded in language. Apel is, however, aware that communicative ethics of a Kantian type is saddled with '*einer ungeheuren Idealisierung*'.[114] This terrible idealizing does not, according to Apel, lead to discourse ethics in itself being wrong. On the contrary, it makes obvious the problem which Apel calls '*der kontrafaktischen Antizipation der idealen Kommunikationsgemenischaft*'.[115] By counterfactual anticipation of the ideal communicative community, Apel means empirically contingent knowledge; that there is a difference between the ideal communicative community as conceived in thought and actual communication and interaction relations, first and foremost conflict relations, which one in fact must anticipate encountering.[116] The question is, what arises with this insight.

One conclusion could be that the transcendental pragmatic justification of communicative ethics sketched above is not generally valid and that communicative ethics should only be seen as a special case of a special ethic in which, through argumentation, interest conflicts are ignored.[117] This solution is rejected by Apel on the simple basis that this would be the same as acknowledging that the argument for discourse ethics put forward above is not viable. Apel reaches a different conclusion, that the justification of discourse ethics presented above is not sufficient for a politically relevant, result-oriented ethic of responsibility. He writes:

> Precisely when one admits its validity, one notices at the same time that there lies, as a precondition to an ideal communicative community, a *counter-factual pre-acceptance*. This pre-acceptance of the *ideal conditions* are unavoidable in the discourse and it necessitates thinking in terms of the principle of validity. But it also contains the admission that in the *real* communicative community, *one should not count on* rationality's ethical foundational norm being followed.[118]

It is precisely the validity of the transcendental pragmatic justification of communicative ethics which, according to Apel, affords the possibility for the anticipation of the ideal conditions for communication, which consists of rational argumentation which freely can be acknowledged by all interested parties. Conceiving the ideal communicative community gives the opportunity to create a distance from the real existing communication. This distance on the one hand hinders an absolutizing of the real existing communication. The communicative community between people *does not necessarily need to* be of a strategic nature. On the other hand, this conception means that people should *not count on* everyone in the communicative community operating on the basis of the ethical norm of dominance-free communication. This communicative ethic has in other words an ethical implication for the practical discourse between people, which makes it possible to relate to it in a normatively distanced way. Practical discourse should not necessarily be of a strategic nature, but it should always be kept in mind that it can be.

Based on this, Apel draws the surprising conclusion that the *responsible* politician *should not* unconditionally choose communication which accords with the ideal situation in communicative ethics. The responsible politician *should* take the real situation into account. The politician is responsible for the *consequences* of his actions. The politician, in other words, is not only faced with communicative ethic's demand for free and dominance-free communication, he is equally confronted with a reality principle which must be taken into consideration. Apel writes:

> He *should* therefore only follow the ideal foundational norm's imperative – for example that power should not be used in consensus oriented conflict resolution – in as much as it does not displace the following of the imperatives

> of the norms of preservation and protection. This paradoxical situation constitutes for him *the problem of applying the ethical foundational norm*. And this problem of application – and not *the ultimate justification of the ideal foundational norm* of the ethic – appears to me to be the primary difficulty in a political *ethic of responsibility*. Here, I have grown accustomed to speak of a 'Part B' of the ethic.[119]

According to Apel, the politician should only follow the demands of communicative ethics, to the extent that they do not disregard the imperatives which political reality set, be they the imperatives to protect, uphold, preserve, etc., the political community. Politicians, according to Apel, are put in the paradoxical situation in that on the one side they are exposed to the imperative to act in accordance with the demands of ideal communicative ethics, while at the same time they *should* ignore these demands in so far as political reality makes this *necessary*. Apel calls this paradoxical situation the application problem of communicative action, which Apel sees as the greatest problem for communicative ethics. The big problem is not the philosophical justification of communicative ethics; this is, according to Apel, possible to overcome.

Apel's formulation can appear surprising because it seemingly pushes ethics aside in preference for the reality principle. It could then always be possible to argue that the reality principle makes it impossible to follow communicative ethic's ideal requirements. It is therefore of decisive importance that Apel resolves this paradox. He writes:

> Justification for an ethic of responsibility, in contrast to an ethic of ultimate ends, gives way in my opinion to the following, granted rather dialectical relationships:
>
> Already as thought, that is to say as argued, we have to stipulate two circumstances: Recognition of the ideal communication community's norm about how to proceed, *and* recognition of its association with an actual, historically developed discursive community. (The latter more precisely means: The recognition of membership in a self-constituting political system which of course can be substituted with another, but which in any case can not be avoided as a "life-basis"). From the dialectical interplay of the two preconditions, of which the one takes only *idealism* into account and the other *realism* and *materialism*, from this interplay between the priviously mentioned two preconditions yields to the implied tension between mutually restrictive norms, which the responsible politician always is obliged to follow.
>
> This, according to my opinion, renders as well *a third norm* between the ideal

> foundational norm and the political reality; and this third norm appears to me to comprise the difference between a political *ethic of responsibility* and a mere *realpolitik* in the meaning of *setting aside morality in preference for purely stretegic thinking*: In that the responsible politician is obliged by this norm to preserve and protect the reality passed on to him, he is in no way relieved of the obligation to the ideal foundational norm and conflict resolution through discursively reaching consensus. Rather, the conflict between the *two* norms yields that the strategically applicabale *third norm* is to be followed: In as much as possible to lead to a long term change in conditions. Change with the longterm goal of lessening the tension between the ideal norm for conflict resolution and the political reality and in this manner move towards the ideal conditions for consensus-oriented conflict resolution.[120]

According to Apel, idealism has always taken as its point of departure the priority of the demand of the ideal, while realism or materialism has always taken as its point of departure the priority of the reality principle. Apel wants to resolve this contradiction in a third principle, which will form the basis of his ethic of responsibility. The principle is that the responsible politician should have the reality principle as his point of departure, which says that he should protect and preserve the social reality which has been entrusted to him. But this obligation does not relieve him of the obligation to follow the fundamental ideal norm that conflict resolution should proceed through the reaching of consensus based on free discussion. This political ethic of responsibility separates Apel from mere 'realpolitik', which has no basis in an ethical principle, but is purely strategic in nature. Apel elaborates this in the following:

> The third norm is as *strategically applicable* as the second norm about preservation and protection, but at the same time it comprises a mediation with the non-strategic foundational norm on discursive consensus reaching. Thus it should only be followed by the responsible politician if purely consensus oriented conflict resolution is not possible. In this case, and only in this case, in domestic politics and to a greater extent in foreign affairs he (the responsible politician) needs a morally founded long term strategy which allows him to employ *instrumental rationality* with respect to other people, with whom a *consensus oriented* 'coordination of action' is not (yet) possible. (On this point it becomes clear that this *ethic of responsibility* differentiates itself, on the one hand from Kant's ethic of ultimate ends, and on the other hand from Max Weber's conception of an *ethic of political responsibility*. This

> difference becomes possible through reflection on three morally relevent implications of the idea of argumentation: 1. the counterfactual pre-acceptance of an ideal communicative community, 2. the actual precondition of real communicative relations, and 3. the practically dictated necessity of progressively eliminating the differences between 1. and 2.[121]

This third norm is, according to Apel, subject to strategic utilization, just as the second norm about the preservation and protection of the communicative community; but it differs from the second norm in that it forms a conduit back to the first basic norm about the dominance-free discussion which is not of a strategic nature. In this way, Apel seeks to create a connection between ethics, which fundamentally is communicative in nature, and political action. Political action, according to Apel, should first and foremost be communicative in character. Only in those cases where it is not (yet) possible to solve political conflicts communicatively, should politicians act strategically in accordance with the third norm, which in the long term aims at creating a situation in which it will be possible to solve conflicts communicatively. This ethic of responsibility sets Apel apart from Kant's ethic of conscience and Weber's political ethic of responsibility. According to Apel, this new formulation of an ethic of responsibility is made possible by rethinking the three implications of the ideal demand of communicative ethics for establishing norms through free, rational argumentation. Communicative ethic's demand for a dominance-free discussion can be anticipated as a regulative idea in relation to the real existing communication, which is tainted by strategic considerations. This contradiction leads to a demand to alter the real existing communication in such a manner that it increasingly comes to approach the ideal of dominance-free communication.

With his ethic of responsibility, Apel has attempted to solve a problem which is apparent in both Kant's ethics of conscience and Weber's political ethic of responsibility. Kant formulated a universal ethic which suffered from the weakness that it was difficult to see how it could be practiced in that which is called real circumstances in Apel's formulation. Kant's ethics stand in direct opposition to the reality principle. In Kant's ethic, human impulses, passions and inclinations are seen as the same as socially institutionalized strategic action, as contingent circumstances which one must abstract from in order to formulate a universal ethic. Kant may be right about this. But the next big problem, as Apel points out, is how such an ethic can be realized in relation to social reality. Kant gives no answer on this issue. Weber takes from Kant his distinction between norm and reality, and in reality increases the discrepancy between norm and reality in as much as he loses Kant's faith in the power and importance of reason in modern society. According to Weber, reason is so stretched and bent by the reality principle in modern society that reason on the social level in Western culture has been transformed into goal-oriented rational action, be it in the form of strategic action or technical-instrumental action. In this way, reason is emptied of its normative references, according to Weber. It has become normless. Weber sees this historical cultural process as the fate of Western society, as it was previously presented. Western culture has basically landed in nihilism. Nihilism, according to Weber, can only be conquered through an heroic action, which consists of deciding to create a normative foundation. But this decision in itself is conditional. Therefore, Weber's political ethic of responsibility is an heroic ethic based on a conception of responsibility which ultimately rests on conditional choices. Weber's political ethic of responsibility is, therefore, not of a universally obligatory character.

The Critical Ethic of Responsibility

The question now is whether Apel has solved the problems which have been shown to afflict Kant's ethics of conscience and Weber's political ethic of responsibility, and then, whether or not Apel has formulated an ethic of responsibility which is of relevance to the ethical situation facing administrators. With regard to Kant's ethics of conscience, Apel has solved an essential problem by transforming Kant's discussion of reason to an issue of linguistic philosophy. Apel presents a convincing argument for communicative reason when he states that it is impossible to argue against communicative reason without what he calls a 'pragmatic self-contradiction' arising.[122] But as previously mentioned, according to Apel, it is not the philosophical justification of communicative reason which contains the greatest problem. The most important problem is the application of the idea of communicative reason in relation to the reality principle, which also, according to Apel, is dominated by strategic rationality. Here Apel is in complete agreement with Weber. Apel has attempted to solve the contradiction between idea and reality by stating that the idea of the ideal communicative community contains a requirement to alter social relations in such a way that domination-free argumentation becomes possible. The thought is good enough. Apel has therefore shown that it is possible to conceive of an ethic of responsibility which has an obligatory relationship to the establishment of norms, and which is not saddled with the arbitrariness which marks Weber's ethic of responsibility. The problem, however, is whether the social reality which is dominated by goal-oriented rational action is contradicted in such a way by the idea of the ideal communicative community that it can be posited that this contradiction of the social reality is *compelling*. It cannot. Not even according to Apel's own theory. In other words, there is an ambiguity in Apel's ethic of responsibility which makes it necessary to elaborate in which way this ethic of responsibility is valid.

The problem in Apel's ethic of responsibility is that it lacks the distinction between negative and positive ethics. By positive ethics I mean an ethic which makes it possible to justify positive actions. By negative ethics I mean an ethic which only makes it possible to justify criticism or objections to a particular way of acting. Apel admits that his ethic of responsibility is not obligatory, in that it must bow to the reality principle. Apel's ethic of responsibility can therefore not be seen as a positive ethic of responsibility. It doesn't have the last word in politics, the reality principle does. Apel's ethic, on the other hand, is a perfectly valid negative ethic. What I mean here is that an objection can always be made against a political action, in that it can always be criticized for not living up to the requirements set forth in Apel's ethic of responsibility. Politics, according to Apel, always stands in relationship to the demands of the ideal communicative situation, but it is not possible to posit a merging of the ideal demands and the political reality. The ideal demand is entirely of a regulative character, which makes it possible to make critical objections to political action. In this understanding of ethics of responsibility, there is a close connection between ethics and critique. An ethic of responsibility can essentially only be of a negative or critical character.[123]

As such, ethics of responsibility are of importance for administrators. The administrator to a much lesser degree than the politician breaks the reality principle because, unlike the politician, he does not set the ultimate goals for his action. On the contrary, he acts in obedience to a number of referents. It is however of decisive importance for the administrator to be able to produce critical objections to the people who give him orders. In this way, a critical ethic of responsibility is relevant for the administrator. This is especially the case when he is presented with contradictory demands, which make it necessary for him to personally make decisions as to how he will act. In this situation, it is of decisive importance that the administrator be able to produce objections against one or another of his referents. The administrator must *have the opportunity to say no*.

Freedom of expression therefore comes to be decisive for the administrator, as he can only put forward his critical objections if he is allowed to. In the next chapter we will treat this issue more closely.

5 Freedom of Expression, the Public Space and Democracy

Freedom of Expression

As stated earlier, the administrator can only put forward his ethically reasoned objections if he is free to do so. Therefore, freedom of expression is of tremendous importance for the administrator. It is, however, not sufficient only to enjoy full *formal* freedom of expression if it is in *reality* not possible to freely express one's positions. Freedom of expression must be realized. Therefore, it is decisive that a public space exists in which freedom of expression can be realized. It is, however, only in a democratic society that freedom of expression can be secured institutionally in a public. Therefore, there is a close connection between ethics, freedom of expression, publicity and democracy. In the following, this connection will be more closely explored.[124]

Freedom of Expression and Publicity

As noted in Chapter 2, full freedom of expression was first formulated in Paragraph 11 of the 1789 Declaration of Human Rights. Paragraph 11 reads:

> The free exchange of ideas and opinions is one of the most valuable human rights. Therefore, each citizen can speak, write and publish freely, under the condition of responsibility for misuse of this freedom in cases laid down by law.[125]

This formulation, in a modified form, has since been incorporated into the Danish Constitution as paragraph 77. This paragraph reads:

> Everyone is entitled to, in print, writing and speech, publicize their thoughts, subject to accountability in a court of law. Censure and other preventative measures can never again be imposed.[126]

From a philosophical perspective, such a formulation expresses the universal in modern society, where language has become central. As mentioned in Chapter 2, Claude Lefort speaks in this context about the transition from the speech of power to the power of speech.

The Greeks had already made this transition.[127] As mentioned in Chapter 1, Aristotle touches on this issue when he writes in *Politics* that what differentiates man from other animals is *logos*. *Logos* means both speech and reason. That which characterizes man is that he is able to express reason through speech. The Greek conception was in principle universal, but in practice restricted. It was only free men who had the right to speak in (the political) public. In his *Politics*, Aristotle gives a long account of why women, guest workers and slaves are denied freedom of expression.

In the Declaration of Human Rights, freedom of expression is universal. It applies to all persons. This did not mean that all persons had freedom of expression in the New Republic which was established after the French Revolution. Women for example were excluded from politics. But this went against the universal aspect of the Declaration. The Declaration can be seen as a regulative idea which demands realization/actualization. When women in France received the right to vote in 1944, this was in principle nothing new in relation to the Declaration. What it was though, was the realization of the universal in modernity which already was formulated in the Declaration.

It is not sufficient merely to declare universal freedom of expression. At the same time, institutions must be created in which expression and speech can take place. In this context I understand institutions very broadly as providing an independent and secure possibility to realize an action of a particular character.[128] One could also say that the possibility for action must be secured for an action to be executed. An institution in which freedom of expression is secured is called a public. The public is freedom of expression's institution.

The Declaration of Human Rights' demand for freedom of expression is not reserved for one single public. The demand for freedom of expression should be understood in such a way that it infers freedom of expression in modern society's many differentiated social contexts and situations. This means that in principle, it should be possible to create a public for freedom of expression in each of these many differentiated social contexts and institutions as soon as there is a need for it. It is precisely in this way that the linguistic oriented modernity described by Habermas is thoroughly infused in modern society's institutions.

The freedom of expression in the manifold institutions should, according to Paragraph 11 of the Declaration, be specified in more detail in law. In Paragraph 77 of the Danish Constitution there is such a detailed specification. This specification is understood to imply that all restrictions on freedom of expression must be justified with reference to the regulative idea, and that eventual restrictions cannot be set arbitrarily. This distinction between principle and real freedom of expression is expressed in legal language as the distinction between formal and material freedom of expression.

Freedom of expression can be summarized as a fundamental political postulate about the individual's right to express himself publicly, which has fundamental philosophical importance and was first codified in the Declaration of Human Rights and then later in the Danish Constitution. Public expression should have the opportunity to be institutionalized in a public. It is first with such institutionalization that one can speak of real freedom of expression. Such an institution can only be created in a modern democratic society.

The Administrator's Paradoxical Freedom of Expression

It is this principal observation which I will, in the following, apply to the administrator's freedom of expression. It is my thesis that the administrator *formally* has the same unrestricted freedom of expression as other citizens, and that their material freedom of expression only has some limitations, which reasonably can be argued for; but despite this, the administrator only has very limited *real* freedom of expression because the administrator's freedom of expression is not institutionally secured in a public.

This thesis is largely unanimously corroborated by the legal literature on the subject. I will not go into details here, but rather point at the major headlines. There is unanimity that the formal freedom of expression which is secured in Paragraph 77 of the Danish Constitution also includes the publicly employed administrator, and that freedom of expression may only be limited if there are special reasons. The problem therefore is to discern the extent of the administrator's freedom of expression. The question must then be addressed through the legal literature. Here, two principally different criteria for limitation are presented. Poul Andersen's 1940 article *Om tjenstemænds ytringsfrihed* (On the civil servant's freedom of expression) deals with clarifying which expressions are illegal.[129] Bent Christensen on the other hand, in his 1980 work *Responsum vedrørende offentligt ansættes ytringsfrihed* (An opinion on the freedom of expression of public employees) has tried to present some criteria for evaluating which expressions are permitted.[130] It appears to be the perspective of Poul Andersen which has dominated the orientation of the more recent literature on the subject. There are also contradictions in this perspective, which I will point out in the following.

It is Poul Andersen's opinion that 'a germane critique, based on correct information of a superior's orders will ... in general be acceptable, on the condition of course that it does not abridge confidentiality'.[131] But on the other hand, a criticism can, according to Poul Andersen, lead to a discretionary dismissal (firing), that is to say, a dismissal based on nothing other than cooperation difficulties: 'Where the right of dismissal is arbitrary, as it is in Denmark, it must be understood that the Minister, without abusing his power can dismiss a civil servant who to a perceptible degree makes cooperation more difficult through such public statements'.[132] In his 1987 book, *Ytringsfrihed. Responsum om offentligt ansættes ytringsfrihed – med særligt sigte på overenskomstansatte DJØF'ere* (Freedom of Expression. An opinion on the freedom of expression of public employees – with special reference to members of 'DJØF'), Nordskov Nielsen reaches a similar conclusion. According to Nordskov Nielsen, there is no real legal basis to restrict freedom of expression. Following this statement there is a big 'but' in Nordskov Nielsen's work: But the eventual ramifications of lawful expressions can lead to punishment or to 'the use of negative sanctions empowered to leadership', which is the euphemism used in legal language.[133]

From a legal perspective, the freedom of expression of the administrator is paradoxical. There is an open contradiction in the administrator's freedom of expression, which prompted Ole Krarup to state in his book *Tjenstemænds ytringsfrihed* (The Civil Servant's Freedom of Expression), that civil servants certainly have freedom of expression, but only on the condition that they don't use it. Krarup expresses this thus:

> ... my main point is that in the hierarchically constructed administration, at no level are public expressions by civil servants allowed which in their content go

> against the authority in question's interests in the broadest understanding (as understood by the authority in question); or expressed in another way: The civil servant has the full freedom of expression elaborated by Poul Andersen, but only under the precondition that it is not used to express direct or indirect criticism of the fundamental circumstances which are accepted or upon which the authority in question's usual praxis and policy are based.[134]

Nordskov Nielsen reaches a similar conclusion in his work cited above, when he writes, 'the importance of rules of law for the administrator's real freedom of expression, are under all conditions, comparatively limited.[135]

The paradox of the administrator's freedom of expression from a legal point of view can be seen as a clash of rules between, on the one hand, the legal rules with regard to freedom of expression and, on the other hand, the legal rules governing the administration's hierarchy of command. On the one hand, there is an overwhelming consensus that there are no limits on the administrator's freedom of expression. On the other hand, as stated above, leadership in the administration can make discretionary firings. This contradiction could from a legal perspective, be solved by establishing legally sanctioned openness and employment and dismissal conditions in the administration. Such an openness could even consist of matters such as employment and dismissals being taken up in a broader and democratically elected forum and that written justifications for both employment and dismissal should be given. There exists already in the present constitution a certain possibility for such a procedure.[136] Such a legally secured procedure could contribute to administrators having the opportunity to freely express themselves without fear of reprisals.

The paradox of the administrator's freedom of expression is not only of a legal character. This becomes clear when a sociological perspective is applied to the administrator's freedom of expression. As mentioned above, public administration is ultimately built upon a hierarchic command structure legally secured in what could be called a public of command. The administrator's freedom of expression, however, is not institutionalized in a legally secured public.

What is of interest from a sociological perspective is that the *lack* or *absence* of such an institutionalized public, for freedom of expression leads to the hierarchy of command public, which is dominated by superiors in the administration all the way down the hierarchy, coming to dominate over the administrator's opportunity to freely express himself within the administration, despite the fact that legally, the administrator should have unlimited freedom of expression within the administration. That which sets the sociological perspective apart from the legal is that the sociological perspective talks about the *absence of an institution* within which the legally secured freedom of expression can be *realized*.

The paradox of the administrator's freedom of expression, from a sociological perspective, can only be solved by creating an institution for freedom of expression for the administrator. Such an institution was called above a *public*. In so much as this public touches the issue of ethics, we can call this an ethical public space.

The Ethical Public Space in Administration

In the ethical public space, all members of the institution should have the opportunity to put forward their objections against specific motions in the administration on an equal basis. In the ethical public space, it should be possible to question the operations of the institution in its widest meaning, be it internal or external and thereby also the norms which form the foundation of the institution.

There are problems, however, associated with constituting an ethical public space. I will only deal with the primary issues here.

The first problem is that such a public space has to be legally secured. Legal rules must be constructed which secure the possibility for the administrator to speak freely within the administrative institution. Formal legal rules giving administrators the opportunity to meet must be created along with procedural rules for how decisions adopted in the ethical public space can be brought to bear on the operation of the institution, including a specification of the status which this space has in relation to the leadership of the administrative institution. The legal problems are surmountable, in that the matter at issue here can be resolved in the usual way, by adopting rules and laws.

The other problem is much larger, in that it entails altering existing social relations. The administrator is socialized into discipline and obedience in the command hierarchy in such a way that he loses his sense for being personally responsible for his actions.[137] The principle of modernity demands personal responsibility for one's actions. In administration, there is an opposite trend, which is that the person disappears in his social role. It is therefore necessary that in administration, a counter socialization process is set in motion which emphasizes the person who bears the social role, rather than the social role which bears the person. Such a socialization towards communicative action and thus ethical discourse can be set in motion in connection with the ethical public space. Within the hierarchic administrative structure, the administrator learns to perform his administrative tasks within the administrative institution. In a similar way, the administrator should have the opportunity, in connection with the ethical public space, to acquire the necessary participatory skills to take a stance on ethical issues which arise within the entire operation of the administration.

The third problem is the largest. This problem has to do with the administrator being interested not only in his own action, but also its implications for the entire administrative institution in which he finds himself. Such an interest can probably only be created if ethical discourse assumes a real importance in relation to the discourse of the command hierarchy. This points in the direction of a long term internal democratization of public administration. What is central here, however, is that such a change is possible because it is in accord with basic principles in modern society. In this context one could even speak of a realization of modernity. I call an administration in which such a living ethical public space is created, an open administration.

The Many Competing Publics

The idea of the open administration constantly runs into the reality principle to such an extent that it may appear unrealistic. We run aground here upon the same issues which plagued communicative action in the previous chapter. It must be accepted that in critical situations the reality principle is stronger than the communicative principle and that the idea of the ethical public space can only be made real as a critical public space. It is also true that neither constitutes a critical public space entirely resistant to the reality principle. The idea of the critical public space only becomes realistic through the idea of many public spaces, which compete with each other and therefore have an interest in reaching into each other's spheres of operation. The idea of many competing public spaces lives up to the reality principle because it is in fact part of modern democratic society, in so much as modern democratic society is built upon pluralism. What is meant by this is that there is a recognition that there may be different interpretations of any situation and that all of these interpretations have an equal right to be put forward in political discussion of the situation, and that the different interpretations can be institutionally anchored in different public spaces. In pluralism lies the principle that different public spaces can exist in society which ensures that one particular interpretation does not come to dominate over all other interpretations. Even though one particular interpretation may dominate in one particular public space, a different interpretation can be found in another public space.

Critique in the ethical public space cannot be grounded in the idea of a higher ethical standard which trumps over the reality principle. Critique can ultimately only be grounded in an interest which is connected to the contradictions in society. But the mediation of the contradictions is dependent upon what institutional opportunities there are for critique. It is in this context that the principle of competing public spaces becomes decisive. The multiple, competing public spaces ensure that different interpretations have the opportunity to be expressed. The more openness there is in administration, the greater the possibility for conflict and cooperation between the different public spaces. This is of importance for the degree of freedom of expression which can be realized, and ultimately, the degree to which democracy can be realized.

The Administrator's Freedom of Expression

The tension between freedom of expression's existence in principle and reality is decisive for the opportunity for an administrator to speak freely in a conflict situation. In this context a number of forms of expression can be delineated, ranging from loyalty to protest and obstruction to exit (*sorti).*[138]

Loyalty is comparable to Weber's ideal type. The loyal civil servant should be prepared to suppress his own personal opinions to carry out an order made by a superior. Loyalty is the fundamental point of departure for the administrator. But it is precisely in situations of conflict between different referents that the administrator cannot be entirely loyal. He is forced to personally make a decision about how he will act. Principally, there are two possibilities for action here. One possibility is for loyalty to be turned into blind obedience, which can take on a pathological character.

The other is for the administrator to resist the order with which he is charged. In this case, there is the possibility for protest, obstruction or exit (*sorti*).

Unconditional obedience towards one's superiors can lead to blind obedience which can ultimately take on a pathological character. A good example of this is Adolf Eichmann, whose obedience is examined in the next chapter.

The other possibility is that the administrator himself takes an independent decision as to how he will act and expresses the reasons for his action in a public space in the administration or in a public space in society in general. Such an action is an example of an ethical action given above. Protest can go to the point where one can speak of direct disobedience. In this case, one can speak of civil disobedience.

The problem for the administrator when it comes to protests is that he singles himself out in protest, thus making himself an easy target for reprisals. The administrator can try to avoid this situation by obstructing an order from a superior. Obstruction has the advantage for the administrator that he can remain anonymous and hereby avoid becoming a victim of reprisals from superiors. Obstruction, however, does not live up to the requirements of being an ethical action. Obstruction is precisely characterized by *not* coming to expression in linguistic form. It therefore cannot raise a discussion which could lead to the justification of other ways of acting in administration.

Exit consists of the administrator leaving his position in protest. This form of protest, however, is very rare. This is the last opportunity for the administrator to be heard if something of monumental importance is at stake for himself or others.

There are then a number of different forms of expression. It should be made clear, however, that it is only protest which lives up to the communicative ethic's demand that social conflicts should be able to be expressed and solved in a public space in modern democratic society.

The Administrator's Obligation to Speak

One could further raise the question as to whether it is possible to shift from the administrator's freedom of expression to his obligation to speak out. It is clear that democracy in general would benefit from administrators who spoke out publicly, as it is they who possess knowledge which is useful in public discussions in society. Democracy lives on these sorts of discussions. One cannot, however, go from freedom of expression for administrators to mandating that they speak out. To do this would be to demand of administrators something which is not demanded of other citizens. But it is a political objective in a democratic society to ensure that the administrator has a genuine opportunity to express his opinions.

Ethics, Freedom of Expression, Publicity and Democracy

There is then a close connection between ethics, freedom of expression, publicity and democracy. The administrator can only resolve his ethical conflicts communicatively if a real freedom of expression in the bureaucracy exists, and freedom of expression can only be secured by institutionalizing it in a public space. Such a public space is not sufficient to secure freedom of expression in administration because ultimately, administration is not governed by communicative rationality. But such an ethical public space can give the opportunity for communication with the many other public spaces in a democratic society. In this way, it should be possible to establish a wider publicity, which subsequently should give the individual administrator a greater chance to exercise his freedom of expression.

In conclusion, the administrator is of great importance in democratic society. The administrator is not just important for the administration of society. By adding to public knowledge about decision making processes, the administrator plays a central role in the practice of democracy in society. In this there must be a political objective in securing freedom of expression for administrators to such an extent that his praxis can realize this fundamental right in society. A circle is thus closed, in which the administrator is dependent upon the general stipulations of democracy, while at the same time contributing to the realization of democracy. This leads to the next chapter which considers more closely the ethical training of the administrator.

6 The Obedient Administrator

The Normative Training of the Administrator

The primary contradiction in ethical conflicts confronting the administrator is that he should act obediently towards his superiors, while at the same time it is he who ultimately is responsible for his actions. The problem then arises as to how the administrator can avoid blind obedience. How can the administrator be in part an authority unto himself, in that he can refuse to comply in situations where such action is necessary? Can the administrative institution be structured in such a manner that such action can be encouraged? Can the individual administrator be trained to act independently when necessary?

All these questions lead to the fundamental question of how it is possible for some people to become obedient tools for others, as is the case in administration. It is in this connection that we will look more closely at the socialization of the administrator. The administrator is socialized to be disciplined and obedient. This pattern of socialization is congruent with the legally oriented, goal-oriented rationality and hierarchical chain of command which characterizes modern administration. Modern administration has the advantage that through this structure a regularity and predictability is created for civil society. The citizen's interaction with the administration should not based upon sex, race or other social group membership. In this way, modern administration promotes the modern stipulation that all people are equal. It is, however, the very same administrative construct which promotes the loss on the part of the administrator of a sense of personal responsibility for his action. In modern society, the principle of personal responsibility for one's action is a fundamental principle, which no one can avoid.[139] This principle is anchored in the legal institutions of modern society. There is then, an internal contradiction in modern administration between obedience and being an authority unto oneself. This leads to the issue of how it is possible on the one hand to resist the tendency for the administrator to obediently disappear into his role, and on the other hand, promote the administrator's personal responsibility. It is this issue which will now be taken up.[140]

The Obedient Administrator

'... the Most Terrible News ...'

Already in the beginning of this century, Max Weber declared the obedience of administrators in bureaucracies to be an historical step forward. This is no longer the case. The obedience of the administrator has itself become a problem. This became increasingly clear after the end of World War II, when we began to see that the tremendous crimes committed in Auschwitz under the Nazi regime were not committed by particularly pathological or criminal elements in society, but rather by normal administrators who believed that they were carrying out the duties of their offices in the bureaucracy.

What is at stake here is a recognition which only very slowly began to gain ground due to the fact that it is associated with the idea that we all could have committed or participated in the great crimes committed under the Nazi regime. Zygmunt Bauman writes in his book *Modernity and the Holocaust* that the most terrible news the Holocaust and its perpetrators brought us is not that 'it' could have happened to us, but rather that we could have carried it out.[141] It is the extremely disquieting element in this acknowledgement that has led to the great resistance in recognizing its validity.

The Holocaust, Bauman writes, has made all (other) memories and surviving conceptions of evil minuscule and insignificant and thereby turned all previously accepted explanations of evil on their head.[142] It suddenly was clear that the most terrible evil humanity could perpetrate was not due to the collapse of social order but, on the contrary, was due to its irreproachable and unchallenged support and persistence. This evil was not the fault of the screaming and unruly mob, but rather obedient and disciplined men in uniform who followed the spirit of rules and its dictates to the letter. It soon emerged that these men, as soon as they took their uniforms off, were in no respect particularly evil. They acted rather like all the rest of us, Bauman writes. They adored their wives, indulged their children, assisted and gave sympathy to their friends when they had problems. It seemed unreal that the same men, when they put their uniforms on shot, gassed or were responsible for the shooting and gassing of thousands of other people, including women, who were the beloved wives of other men and children who were other people's beloved children. This was what was horrendous. 'How could ordinary people like you and I do these kinds of things?', asks Bauman.[143]

The Authoritarian Personality

The thought that these people could be just like us has been so intolerable that the first research on the crimes of Nazism rested on the idea that the perpetrators must have been particular, special, or somehow different from us. They must have escaped in some way the influence of civilized society, or in some way or another have been perverted or corrupted by the influence of some form of evil; an unfortunate combination of socialization factors which resulted in a defective, sick personality.

Adorno put forward such an understanding in his book *The Authoritarian Personality* which he wrote with a research team in the United States and published after the end of the Second World War.[144] The primary thesis in this book was the idea that Nazism was built upon a particular personality type, which Adorno calls 'the authoritarian personality'. This personality is characterized by its tendency towards obedience towards those who are stronger and higher up, and by their scrupulous and gruesome feelings of superiority over the weak. The triumph of Nazism in Germany was thus a result of the authoritarian personality being particularly strongly represented in Germany.

Bauman criticizes Adorno's investigation in *Modernity and the Holocaust* in the following way:

> The fashion in which Adorno and his team articulated the problem was important not so much because of the way in which blame was apportioned, but because of the bluntness with which all the rest of mankind was absolved.[145]

Bauman's criticism is essential because it questions the indirect implication of Adorno's thesis that all of us who do not have an authoritarian personality are acquitted. According to Bauman, Adorno divides the world up into people born pro-Nazi and their victims. The disquieting knowledge that many friendly people can be evil if required is thereby suppressed. The suspicion that even the victims could lose a great deal of their humanity on the way to perdition was, according to Bauman, taboo.[146] Bauman further criticizes Adorno for looking exclusively at the personal character of individuals, instead of also bringing into his analysis the social conditions that could produce the authoritarian personality.

Bauman exaggerates when he claims that Adorno is not interested in the creation of the authoritarian personality. But the central point in Bauman's critique is important. In that blame is placed on some, there are simultaneously others who are guilt-free. Evil has been demarcated and is therefore capable of being dealt with. It is this postulate which has since been contested.

Eichmann in Jerusalem

In this connection, Hannah Arendt's interpretation of the prosecution of Adolf Eichmann in Jerusalem in 1961 is important. Arendt was a reporter at the trial of Eichmann and collected her writings in the famous, and notorious, book *Eichmann in Jerusalem.*[147] The book bears the subtitle 'A Report on the Banality of Evil'. This brings us to the thesis that awoke great contempt when the book came out; Eichmann was an entirely ordinary man, who led a normal family life and did his job as an administrator in the German bureaucracy.

In her reporting, Arendt shows that Eichmann was not exceptional in the Third Reich. He was, rather, symptomatic of the general moral collapse which Nazism not only brought out in Germany, but in all of Europe, not just among executioners, but also among the victims.[148] As Eichmann saw it, no one, not one individual spoke out against the '*Endlösung*'. On the contrary, everybody cooperated. Even the victims, even the Jews, worked on organizing the journey to their own funeral.[149] '*Immerzu fahren hier die Leute zu ihrem eigen Begräbnis*'. 'Continuously, people travel from here to their own funeral' wrote a Jewish observer in Berlin in 1943.[150] As Arendt wrote, there was no voice from the outside which could awaken Eichmann's conscience. The 'respectable class in society' which Eichmann tried to live up to all his life, either assented or remained silent.[151] 'No one, absolutely no one, came to me and decried anything which had to do with the carrying out of my duties' testified Eichmann at his trial.[152]

Eichmann had good reason to feel like Pontius Pilate, concludes

Arendt.[153] But as the months and years went by, he lost the need to feel anything at all. Everything he did, he did as a law abiding citizen. It was as things should be, it was the law of the land, which was based on the word of the Füher. According to his own testimony, he did his job, he didn't just act upon orders but acted in accordance to the law.[154]

According to Arendt, Eichmann was capable of seeing this moral collapse.[155] During the trial, when he was confronted with the proposition that he carried out orders of a criminal nature, he himself made the distinction between obeying orders and obeying the law. He was not himself '*Kadavergehorsam*', or blindly obedient. It was in this context that Eichmann, to everyone's astonishment, began to speak of Kant's moral philosophy. According to his own statements, Eichmann believed that he always lived up to Kant's moral prescriptions, especially in accordance with Kant's definition of 'duty'. The judge found this astonishing because Kant's understanding of duty stands in sharp contrast to blind obedience, which according to Arendt's opinion, was the widespread understanding in the court of Eichmann's way of acting. In answer to Judge Raveh's question, Eichmann was able to give a rather correct definition of Kant's Categorical Imperative: 'I meant by my remark about Kant that the principle of my will must always be such that it can become the principle of general law'.[156] As a point of clarification, Arendt adds that Kant's principle does not encompass robbery and murder, because the robber and murderer cannot desire a society in which it is lawful to rob and murder him. It became apparent from the next question that Eichmann had read Kant's *Kritik der praktischen Vernuft*. Eichmann then explained that from the moment when he began to carry out the 'Endlösung', he ceased to live according to Kant's Categorical Imperative. He himself was conscious of this, but comforted himself with the thought that he was 'no longer the master of his own actions' and that he was not capable of changing anything'.

Arendt comments upon the testimony that in the period when the state, in Eichmann's own words 'had legalized criminal action', Eichmann did not just reject Kant's Categorical Imperative as inapplicable. Eichmann had, according to Arendt's opinion, also altered Kant's principle to an imperative that the principle upon which one should act is the same principle upon which the law of the land is based. Hans Frank, the Nazi governor of Poland further deformed Kant's Categorical Imperative, which became the categorical imperative for the Third Reich, which Arendt believed Eichmann must have been familiar with, to read: 'You should act in such a way that the Füher, would approve of your actions if he knew about them'.[157] Arendt's opinion is that Kant had never said anything like this. On the contrary, every person makes law as soon as he begins to act, and it is by using his practical reason that the individual finds the principle which can or should be the fundamental principle for the law. But Arendt concurs with Eichmann in that his unconscious bending of the Categorical Imperative is in accordance with what Kant meant by his account of what the ordinary person could deal with in relation to moral action. In his *Kritik der praktischen Vernuft*, Kant differentiates between the philosopher and an ordinary person with regard to moral judgement. He writes:

> However, when asked where this pure virtue might exist that we might test, as with testing an iron, the moral values of each action, I must admit that only philosophers might, without a doubt make such a decision, because in the understandings of mere men, these questions are not derived at through common rules, but indeed through common usage, in the same way as the usage of the right or left hand.[158]

The ordinary person who discerns practically rather than based upon general principles should, according to Kant, go a step further than merely obeying the law and ask: 'Is this action carried out on the basis of moral law and not just because it is virtuous and correct as an action itself, but also because it has moral value as a maxim for the disposition of the person?[159] The only thing remaining from the spirit of Kant's Categorical Imperative, according to Arendt, is the demand that it is not sufficient for the ordinary person to be law abiding; he must also go beyond the demand for blind obedience and identify his own will by the principle that could become the basis for law, the source from which law springs.[160] Arendt then states that in Kant's philosophy, the source is practical reason, while with Eichmann, the source is the will of the Füher. Much of 'the terrible, conscientious, thoroughness' of the 'Endlösung' can, according to Arendt, be traced back to the curious view, which according to her estimation is normal for Germans and the consummate bureaucrat, that abiding by the law does not just mean abiding by the law, but acting as if one was the legislator oneself of the law which one obeys. From this, according to Arendt, comes the ordinary German belief that nothing less than going beyond obligation and internalizing the law as one's own is demanded.[161]

It is clear that Kant's idea of practical reason is distorted out of recognition in Arendt's presentation of it. But Arendt does not consider whether this distortion can be traced back to Kant's own philosophy. I believe that it can because Kant differentiates between philosophers and ordinary people, and then rejects the idea that the reason of ordinary people should be sufficient to derive action from general principles. In this way, Kant's philosophy opens itself up for the type of perversion met in the Eichmann case. This appears to be Arendt's own opinion as well, which she has great difficulty accepting. It is, however, a matter which can illustrate my proposition. This has to do with the requirement of obedience for civil servants discussed above in Max Weber's *Politik als Beruf*: 'The honor of the functionary is the ability to carry out an order on the demand and responsibility of a superior, even against personal sympathy, as conscientiously as if the order was his own conviction'.[162] In light of this quote, it is easy to see the direct line from Kant's ordinary human reason through Weber's obedient civil servant to Eichmann's duty-bound obedience towards orders and the law.

Arendt notes that Eichmann did his best to carry out the 'Endlösung' and that he proceeded all the way up to 1945, when largely everyone in the German administration dropped this ambition and went to work trying to cover over all traces of it.[163] The only possibility for the judges to understand Eichmann's behavior was that Eichmann either had an unbridled hate of Jews, or that he must have lied to the court when he declared that he always followed orders. The judges saw no other possibilities and therefore, according to Arendt, never understood Eichmann. According to Arendt, he was not driven by a hatred of Jews; rather, he was driven by his conscience. Arendt supports this by noting that Eichmann knew towards the end of the war that Hitler wanted the death mill at Auschwitz to continue, and that Himmler therefore acted against the wishes of the Füher when he tried to dismantle and cover over the traces of Auschwitz.[164] When Eichmann was confronted in Jerusalem with his extraordinary obedience to Hitler and his orders, according to Arendt, he repeatedly tried to explain by saying '*Führerworte haben Gesetzekraft*', that 'the word of the führer has law-making power'. This meant, among other things, that an order from Hitler didn't necessarily have to be written. Therefore, Eichmann never asked to see a written order from Hitler. Such written orders probably were never issued. But Hitler's word formed the foundation for the formulation of the legal basis for the 'Endlösung'.

Arendt summarizes her presentation by declaring that civilized countries are built upon that law we know from the Ten Commandments, that we must not kill. But in the Third Reich, Hitler introduced the law that 'you must kill'.[165] Evil thereby lost its tempting character as that which we must not do. Temptation in the Third Reich was to *not* kill, to *not* steal, to *not* let one's neighbor travel to his own funeral. Evil, in Arendt's words became banal.

Milgram's Experiment: Unlimited Obedience

The Experiment

Arendt's book led to so much outrage because it nakedly showed how evil could take on a banal character. In this way, evil became uncontrollable. Eichmann, according to Arendt's analysis, was not just a vile criminal, he was also a completely ordinary law abiding civil servant, who carried out his duties in accordance with the orders he received from his superiors in the bureaucracy. Eichmann was an ideal-typical administrator in Max Weber's bureaucratic machine. In this frightening perspective, it is obvious to ask whether Eichmann's obedience was due to the fact that he was in the administration of the Nazi's state apparatus, or whether it is the case that obedience in general has no limits. It is this question which Stanley Milgram raised in his investigation *Obedience to Authority*.[166]

Milgram illustrated this question through a series of psychological laboratory experiments, where he investigated the extent to which ordinary people voluntarily would obey an authority and, on his order, administer an electrical shock through another person to promote that person's learning of a series of words. Milgram is aware that there is a great difference between an experiment in a laboratory and the forms of obedience encountered under Nazism. But the essence of obedience to Milgram is the same.[167] This consists of the individual coming to see himself as a tool for carrying out the will of another person, and therefore no longer seeing himself as responsible for his actions. Once an individual gives himself over to an authority and no longer sees himself as the source of his own actions then, according to Milgram, the way is paved for all the essential traits of obedience, such as the adaptation of thought and the will to follow, even in carrying out gruesome acts on command. It is the principle of obedience which is decisive. What is not significant to Milgram is whether this obedience takes place in one environment or another. Therefore, it should be possible to investigate people's tendency towards obedience in a laboratory. It was Arendt's interpretation of Eichmann which led Milgram to this perspective. People participated voluntarily in the laboratory experiment and were in no way forced to comply. This accords with the principle understanding of obedience, in which obedience is a voluntary action. Once the participants in the experiment gave up their authority and attached themselves voluntarily to the authority of the experiment leader, Milgram's experiment consisted of observing at what point the participant appeared to try to regain his authority as he was ordered to administer an increasingly strong current to the student on the other end, and thereby carrying out increasingly gruesome actions.

The results of Milgram's investigation are not encouraging. The participants in the experiments displayed an obedience which exceeded all expectations. The majority of the participants acted in obedience to the experiment leader and administered what they believed to be very high shocks to the student on the other side. There were very few who displayed direct disobedience and stopped the experiment. The experiment showed that obedience is a dominant characteristic in people. People who deeply reject theft, killing and violence can, according Milgram, be easily induced to preform such actions with relative ease under the command of an authority.[168] A behavior which is unthinkable to an individual acting on his own is easily carried out if it is ordered. The gruesome actions, according to Milgram, are not linked to the individual himself, but rather in the social relations to authority. In this connection, Milgram speaks of the individual being brought into an instrumental situation, in distinction to when he acts independently or autonomously. Milgram defines this agentic state as the condition in which the individual sees himself as an instrument carrying out another person's will.[169] In this condition, the person is open to control by a person of higher status. The individual no longer sees himself as responsible for his actions, but defines himself as a tool in carrying out another's wishes.

Another important result of the Milgram tests is that the agentic state can be rationalized technically and perfected, and that such rationalization and perfection increases the possibilities of carrying out gruesome actions. Under the right research conditions, only 35% of the participants in the study refused to administer the strongest shock, 'level 30' containing what was believed to be 450 volts, to the student on the other side to encourage the student to learn a list of words.[170] This result may appear trivial, but it is not. Milgram conducted a survey of psychiatrists, students and adults from the middle class to see how they believed they would react if they participated in the experiment. It is indicative that all those surveyed believed that they would refuse to obey the experiment leader at a very early stage in the experiment and believed that nearly everyone would refuse to comply in administering shock-level 9, at 135 Volts. They believed that only a very marginal group would administer shock-level 20, at 300 Volts.[171] No one could imagine that anyone would administer shock-level 30, at 450 Volts, which in fact 65% of the participants in the experiment did under special conditions.

In relation to the actual results of Milgram's experiment it is important to note that none of the survey respondents could imagine that they themselves could have done what the participants in the experiment actually did. Milgram explains this difference as the difference between being in an autonomous versus an agentic state.

As noted above, the agentic state can be rationalized. Milgram found that there was an inverse relationship between carrying out gruesome acts and closeness to the victim.[172] It is easiest to harm a person who one can neither see nor hear. It is more difficult when one can hear the victim, even more difficult when one can see the victim, and most difficult when one personally must inflict pain on the victim. When the 'student' could neither be seen nor heard, 65% of the participants in the experiment applied the highest voltage level. When the participants could hear the victim, compliance dropped to 62.5%. When the participants could see the victim, compliance dropped to 40%. When the participant actually had to place the victims hand on the contact point for the electrical shock, compliance dropped to 30%. Seeing the victim was the factor that played the most important role in whether or not the participant continued with the experiment.

Milgram concludes that every factor or event which is placed between the experiment participant and the victim leads to a reduced psychological burden on the participant and therefore increased compliance.[173] According to Milgram, what characterizes modern society is that there usually are other people between the individual and the final destructive action to which the individual contributes. According to Milgram, this holds also for modern bureaucracy, as well as when it is established for a destructive end, as was the case in Nazi Germany. Most of the people in the Nazi bureaucracy were preoccupied with basic tasks and not with the ultimate destructive character of the bureaucracy's ends. Rather, they undertook a series of discrete tasks which made the ultimate destructive action possible. Lists of the victims and their property were to be made, they were to be transported in freight trains, the locomotive needed water, etc.

Milgram also took this issue into account in his experiment.[174] In one of the experiments, the participant in the experiment no longer actually pressed the button administering the shock. The participant would only order another to press the button. The number of people who then complied rose to 92.5%. Only 7.5% of the participants declined to administer the maximal shock of 450 volts. Milgram concluded that it is possible for any leader or group of leaders to create a bureaucracy with the aim of carrying out gruesome acts by only involving the most unfeeling and insensitive people to carry out the directly destructive actions. The largest proportion of the people in the bureaucracy usually, due to their distance from the actual violent actions, will only feel slight misgiving about carrying out their supporting functions. They are therefore likely to feel that they bear no responsibility for the actions in question in two ways. First, it is the legitimate authority in the bureaucracy that vouches for their actions, and secondly, it is not they themselves who carry out the physically violent actions.[175] With the division of labor and chain of command in modern bureaucracy, not only rationality, effectiveness and economizing in administration is promoted, but also the possibility to carry out gruesome actions.

The Creation of the Agentic State

Milgram proceeds to consider why obedience exists at all.[176] In this connection, he concentrates on the transition from the autonomous to the agentic state. In this context, Milgram considers three circumstances. The first has to do with the conditions for a person moving from the autonomous to the agentic state. The second has to do with the consequences of the transition to the agentic state, that is to say, what behavioural and psychological characteristics are changed within the person. The third has to do with what keeps a person in the agentic state.

With regard to the first issue, having to do with the conditions for entering the agentic state, Milgram emphasizes general socialization to obey authorities. This socialization has to do with both primary socialization in the family and secondary socialization in the institutional authority systems, which in modern society are primarily characterized by their impersonal nature.[177] These authority systems are internalized by reward and punishment. These circumstances, however, only comprise the general prerequisites for the transition to the agentic state.[178] The direct prerequisite is that the person in question acknowledges and recognizes an authority when entering a psychological experiment. The power of authority does not arise from personal characteristics, but rather the position one ascribes the authority in the social structure. In that the authority is acknowledged as relevant, in this case for the carrying out of the experiment, the authority is acknowledged voluntarily not just as an external authority, but also as an internal authority, whom it is right to obey. This obedience can then be supported by an ideology which in this case is the ideology of serving scientific progress within pedagogy. The authority of the experiment leader is based on the participants giving their voluntary assent. When this assent is first given, according to Milgram, it is difficult to withdraw it again.

The Consequences of the Agentic State

The second issue which Milgram takes up is the behavioural and psychological changes that occur in the person when he comes under the authority of another person in the agentic state. What is important here is that the participant in the experiment directs his attention towards the experiment leader's authority, and then binds and aims himself at competently realizing the commands made by the authority.[179] The participant in the experiment follows the instructions of the experiment leader, he concentrates on the purely technical way in which the shock is administered, and becomes entirely preoccupied by the narrow technical task which lies before him. The punishment of the student recedes increasingly into the background until it becomes an insignificant part of the total experience, it becomesa minor phenomenon amongst the complicated activities in the laboratory, as it is defined by the experiment leader who has legitimate authority.

At this point we reach one of the most extensive consequences of the transition to the agentic state.[180] In this condition, the participant feels himself responsible to the authority who guides him; but he does not feel responsible for the *content* of the actions which the authority requests of him. According to Milgram, morality does not disappear, it just takes an entirely different reference point. The participant feels pride or shame depending upon how correctly he carries out the actions the authority tells him to.[181] This is the decisive finding in Milgram's experiment that puts the whole experiment in perspective. Morality does not disappear! It is just put in a different perspective. The participant does not lose his morality, when he enters the agentic state. What happens is that morality becomes based on the authority rather than the person himself.

Again we are back to the decisive realization which Arendt reached in her analysis of Eichmann, and which Milgram uncovers on an experimental basis. Eichmann was not without morals, as most people wanted to believe. On the contrary, as Arendt stated, he acted morally, and he himself saw his actions as moral. But Eichmann's morality became banal because it was based in an authority other than his own. In Eichmann's case, it was based ultimately in the person of Hitler. In Milgram's experiment, the morality of the participant was rooted in the morality of the experiment leader. According to Milgram, this authority figure is general. But in bureaucracy, it is systematically cultivated. This becomes the very principle of rational authority in bureaucracy, as it also is formulated by Weber.

In *Modernity and the Holocaust*, Zygmunt Bauman gives an eminent analysis of Milgram's experiment in which he highlights the finding that the bureaucratic authority system, contrary to the broadly accepted notion, does not go against moral norms as such, and does not reject them as a fundamentally irrational, emotional factor which works against truly effective, dispassionate rationality.[182] On the contrary, the bureaucratic authority system uses moral norms in a new form. The great achievement of bureaucracy consists of its moralization of technology in combination with a denial of the moral significance of non-technical fields.[183] According to Bauman, it is the technology of action, not its objective or goal, which is judged to be good or bad, appropriate or inappropriate, right or wrong.[184] It is in evaluating ends then that moral evaluation is brought in, in as much as each decision includes a normative dimension. The objective of the action is thus excluded from normative evaluation. But again, it must be underlined that the objective of the action is only excluded from normative evaluation in so far as the evaluation is passed on to what Bauman calls foster conscience. This foster conscience is characterized precisely by being localized in authority, which steps in in place of the participant in the experiment's own conscience. The frightful thing about Milgram's experiment, among other things, is that in the hour which was set aside for each participant, it was possible to build up a foster conscience of such strength that 92.5% of all participants, under rather special circumstances, were willing to administer the maximal shock. But these 'rather special circumstances' are very common circumstances in a bureaucracy; they are called the division of labor. Division of labor is the general characteristic of a bureaucracy to such an extent that it is hardly comparable to the primitive division of labor in the experiment, where one person is to ask another to push a button. The foster conscience in the experiment was based on the idea that the experiment was to promote scientific knowledge. When one of the participants began to protest about sending a stronger current through the student, the experiment leader replied 'The experiment requires that you continue'.[185] The participant then asked 'Do you take responsibility?', to which the leader responded, 'The responsibility is mine, that is true. Please continue'. With such notification, the participant continued to apply 450 Volts for each wrong answer.

The participant becomes morally bound to the experiment leader or authority's foster conscience in a way which can be expressed in the concepts of 'loyalty', 'duty' and 'discipline'. It is through one's moral attachment to authority that authority receives its moral power over the experiment participant to the extent that authority can come to play the role of foster conscience. In this way, the participant loses understanding of his actions. In the experiment this was expressed frequently by a number of participants in the statement, 'If it was up to me, I wouldn't have shocked the student'.[186] The moral demands which lie in loyalty to authority and duty to carry out the orders of authority with discipline replace the person's personal morality and ultimately make the person into the subject of another. Milgram rightly calls this condition a spiritual condition, which creates the conditions for having a person act in obedience to the orders of another, without taking a stance on the content of the order.[187]

The Binding Power of the Agentic State

This brings us to Milgram's third issue; what it is that keeps people in the agentic state? Milgram has several explanations for this.[188] Initially, it has to do with the person being slowly drawn into a series of actions, a sequence of actions in which one leads to another and so on. It would not be possible for the participant to stop the sequence without reconsidering his own actions. If the participant stopped, according to Milgram, he would have to say, 'Everything that I have done up to this point is evil, and I acknowledge this by stopping'. In this understanding, the participant is imprisoned in his own actions. Milgram adds another explanation to this which he calls situational obligations.[189] What Milgram means by situational duties is that each social situation is supported by mutual recognition of the social status of the different social agents. The experiment leader has, from the start, a social status which the participant will not reject by not complying as the experiment continues. Zygmunt Bauman supports this explanation in *Modernity and the Holocaust*.[190] I, however, do not believe this explanation to be sufficient. First, it is based on a fear of realistically looking at one's own actions; secondly, it builds upon a general view of the constitution of the social. In my opinion, a better explanation is that the participant actively passes on his responsibility to the authority's foster conscience and that the actions thereby, according to the perspective of the participant, are seen as continuous actions carried out by the authority. To stop would be the same as stopping the actions of the authority. As the participant has passed on his personal moral power to the foster conscience, he no longer has the power to intervene in the actions of the authority, which from a general moral consideration are the participant's own actions. The agentic state is thus populated by morally incapacitated persons. It is this incapacitation which prohibits these persons from acting on their own.

Strain and Disobedience

In this context, one can ask what at all can make a person break from the agentic state and act disobediently towards the authority of the experiment leader? Milgram points out that it is not sufficient to explain disobedience morally, as seen morally it may be equally immoral to send an electric shock, regardless of how near or far away the victim is, but that obedience and disobedience varies according to how far removed the victim is. Milgram would then rather speak of the level of strain to which the participant is subjected.[191] What Milgram means by strain is *externally originating irritations* which impact and disturb the person in the agentic state. Strain is a sign that authority does not have full control over the participant in the experiment. The source of strain for the participant could be screams from the student, the feeling of moral violation in inflicting pain on another person, the division between the experiment leader's and the student's directions or an unwillingness to hurt another person.[192] What is interesting, however, is that such irritations do not directly lead to disobedience. On the contrary, most of the participants reacted to these irritants through psychological mechanisms which constructed a form of spiritual protection which Milgram calls cognitive adjustment.[193] Here, the participant can attempt to avoid seeing realistically what he has done, or even deny it. Some participants attempted to send a milder shock or for a shorter duration than was prescribed by the experiment leader, or tried to report sending a stronger shock than they actually did. But none of these actions led to direct disobedience towards the experiment leader. Milgram interprets these actions as attempts by the participant to avert taking personal responsibility for his actions. In this postulate, Milgram is supported by the fact that when stress is increased, the participant asks for direct assurance that it is the experiment leader who bears responsibility. In this connection, Milgram cites a clarifying example from the experiment. Under great stress, the participant has reached 375 Volts, whereupon the following dialogue takes place:

> Teacher (experiment's subject): I think something is happening to that fellow in there. I don't get no answer. He was hollering at less voltage. Can't you check in and see if he's all right, please?
> Experimenter (*same detached calm*): Not once we've started. Please continue, Teacher.
> Teacher (*sits down, sighs deeply*): 'Cool – day, shade, water, paint.' Answer please. Are you all right in there? Are you all right?
> Experimenter: Please continue, Teacher. Continue please (*Teacher pushes button*).
> Teacher (*swivelling around in his chair*): Something's happened to that man in there. (*Swivelling back*) Next one. 'Low – dollar, necklace, moon, paint.' (*Turning around again*) Something's happened to that man in there. You had better check in on him, sir. He won't answer or nothing.
> Experimenter: Continue. Go on, please.
> Teacher: You accept all responsibility?
> Experimenter: The responsibility is mine. Correct. Please go on. (*Teacher returns to his list, starts running through words as rapidly as he can read them, works through to 450 volts.*)
> Teacher: That's that.[194]

At this point, the psychic sources of strain can change and manifest themselves in physical symptoms which then can have a mitigating impact. The participant could, for example, begin to shake, sweat, etc. In the final stage, according to Milgram, dissent can arise, which means that the participant protests in different ways to the experiment leader, without actually stopping the experiment. All of the mechanisms described, according to Milgram, serve to keep the participant's relation to authority in tact in that the conflict experienced is reduced to an acceptable level.[195]

Dissent can take different forms which may result in threats of non-compliance. What is important here, however, is that disobedience is not just a matter of an action continuing from previous actions. Rather, it is a matter of overturning the established social relations between the experiment leader and the participant in the agentic state. The problem with a disobedient act is that the entire moral order needs to be overturned, in that the participant recovers his conscience and takes personal responsibility for his actions. At this point, the experiment may actually be stopped. The experiment cannot be maintained if the person begins to take responsibility for his actions. According to Milgram, if the participant acts disobediently, he believes that he has ruined the experiment, he works against the goal of the researcher, and he shows that he is in disagreement with the task he has been given. It is precisely at this point that Milgram says the participant puts into use the measure which we were looking for and affirms humanistic value norms.[196]

Evaluating Milgram's Experiment

Milgram's experiment is valuable because it uncovers, in experimental form, obedience's voluntary character, which Arendt already displayed in the Eichmann case. But in the Eichmann case, so many particular historical factors of a coercive and ideological nature were present, making it possible to reject Arendt's horrifying portrayal of the banality of evil. It could be that Eichmann carried out his duties primarily because he was a Nazi. If we accept this, we can relax as long as our society is not controlled by a Nazi state. But the instant we accept Arendt's interpretation that Eichmann carried out his duties primarily because he was an exemplary, disciplined and loyal bureaucrat, the result is also disturbing in a democratic society. Milgram's experiment supports this latter interpretation of Eichmann, in that the participants acted obediently voluntarily. It is, therefore, difficult to reject his results, which uncover the fundamental principle of obedience.

When obedience is brought into a social context, isn't the principle of obedience weakened? On the contrary, it is strengthened. This is the most disturbing result. In his experiment, Milgram was not only historically inspired by Arendt. He was also inspired by the Vietnam War, where very normal Americans were willing to carry out the most gruesome acts. Milgram compared the transcripts from the trial of Eichmann with the transcripts from the trial of the soldiers who carried out the massacre in the civilian village of My Lai in Vietnam.[197] There is an astounding similarity between the obedience in the two cases. This was a case where a group of people carried out their jobs, in which they were more influenced by administrative norms than personal moral norms. All the participants entered the agentic state, in which none took responsibility for their actions, but rather referred further to others. The organization itself becomes a responsibility dissolving instrument, which Bauman indicates in his interpretation of Milgram's experiment.[198] Responsibility becomes fluid. The individual is then bound by norms such as loyalty, duty and discipline to the organization's hierarchy.[199] A further linguistic modification of action takes place, in that personal morality is spared and the person lower in the hierarchy pushes responsibility upwards, at the same time that the action is justified ideologically. In Vietnam, for example, Americans fought against the 'Red Menace'. Obedience rarely takes on an heroic character. Actors act neither with a strong conscience, nor are they possessed by strong aggression. They are, according to Milgram, first and foremost functionaries, who have a job to do, and try to create the impression in others, not least their superiors, that they carry out their work conscientiously and skillfully.

At the end of his book, Milgram asks where the outermost limit of obedience is. There is no limit to obedience! This is his disturbing message.

Slotsholmen

'In Denmark, nothing is as great as in the great wide world beyond – this should be the self-satisfaction of all Danes', writes the author and civil servant Ulrich Horst Petersen in the beginning of his essay *På Slotsholmen* (On Slotsholm).[200] Fortunately, we cannot produce for display an Eichmann, and Milgram's experiment took place all the way on the other side of the Atlantic. It may be necessary, therefore, to say that the phenomena which are described above are also found in Danish administration. To illustrate this, I will use a literary, a theoretical, and a practical example from Slotsholmen.

On Slotsholmen

In his essay on Slotsholmen, Ulrich Horst Petersen describes a civil servant who entirely lives up to Milgram's description of the agentic state. For this particular civil servant, the whole system is about ascending and getting a share of power. 'There is nothing peculiar about this' Horst Petersen writes. 'The whole system the civil servant works in points in one direction: Upwards. One bows one's head, but that is because one strives upwards. Towards a higher wage, but also towards the manager role and the importance it has in the system. The latter is possibly more important than the former. The wage hardly motivates many people to 'go in for the career', no, it's surely the importance of the role which attracts'.[201] Horst Petersen then describes what happens to the civil servant when he takes on the role. The civil servant very easily plays the role and thereby becomes one with the role. As a person, he can have less or completely lose contact with his family. They know and accept him only as a person, and he cannot expect to advance in the family in the same way as at the office. The civil servant can also lose contact with himself. According to Horst Petersen, this can for example come to expression as a loss of connection to one's own dreams:

> I simply discovered that I could no longer remember what I dreamt. I had been employed a while, when it finally hit me that my dreams, which before were living and vibrant, now were pale, dull and said nothing – yes, saying nothing as if there was nothing to say, or that which there was to say must not be said. ... There was something about these almost insulting nothing-saying dreams (or: dreams that say nothing), which reminded me of the papers, deliberations and reports I sat and read in there. They were, to a certain extent, no longer mine, as I was about to teach my subconscious this language, or more correctly: Slotsholmen was about to become a part of my unconscious nature. They say that when one begins to dream in a foreign language, one has mastered it. But with Slotsholmen its the opposite: When you begin to dream in the language of Slotsholmen, it has mastered you. It has become one's second nature.[202]

Horst Petersen then describes how the whole of human spontaneity is suppressed, in that the person becomes totally enveloped in the role, which has its place in the pyramid of power. Language itself in this connection takes a pyramidic character. The lower strata, Horst Petersen says, endeavor to agree with what the higher strata say, even in what they think, as they already have patterned their way of thinking after the way the higher strata thinks, which affords a reasonable chance to win the approval of the higher strata as they think just like each other.[203] In this way, according to Horst Petersen, the higher strata's images and their images of their own excellence, are confirmed, which is not only dangerous for themselves and their own judgement, but also for the administration, because criticisms of their actions and situation are harder to express (become increasingly less likely) the closer one gets to the top. When no one dares say what they believe, but only what they believe everyone else of importance believes, according to Horst Petersen, the importance of beliefs diminishes in relation to who has the belief, and it doesn't make it any easier to defend the power pyramid by alluding to it as a guarantee for objectivity.[204] Horst Petersen sees the problem as lying in this pyramidic organization of human life itself, which occurs everywhere in society when organizations reach a certain size.[205]

Horst Petersen makes no proposals for how we might be able to rid ourselves of the pyramidic organization of people. His advice to one who wants to retain his judgement is almost stoical: 'Naturally, a civil servant must live in his own era, if he can, but he can only evade being a civil servant if he really allows the role and the sweetness of power to run away with him – and then he will really be led by the nose'.[206] According to Horst Petersen, civil servants have a reputation for being 'skeptical and ironic and not all too active'. The latter, according to Horst Petersen, is a defamation. It is probably correct if you take the expression as a comment on work activity. But the expression can also be read along with skepticism and irony as a moral virtue in the Stoic's moral code. Horst Petersen's advice is for the civil servant to retain his personal interface with his role. This cannot be done if one is subsumed in the role; it can only be achieved if one retains some distance from it. Skepticism and irony here are the Stoic's medicine. Moderate activity follows from this. Maybe it wasn't for nothing that Seneca was an administrator in the court of Emperor Augustus.[207] But the problem remains; who will be the department chief, when all the new candidates in the central administration become stoics?

Ulrich Horst Petersen himself abdicated from a manager's chair with its accompanying carpet, to live by the moral code of the stoics: 'Happy is he who lives unnoticed'. It is still the roles and the agentic state which set the norm on Slotsholmen. This is also the irony in Ulrich Horst Petersen's skepticism.

Covert Disciplining

In 1981, a group of civil servants from Slotsholmen anonymously presented a report with the title *Den skjulte disciplinering* (Covert Disciplining) which in a different genre reaches the same diagnosis of life on Slotsholmen. In this report, they pose themselves the question of how a new civil servant can be disciplined and whether he has the chance to resist this disciplining and still remain a civil servant.[208] The report is based upon observations from the Danish Ministry of Justice and Ministry of Foreign Affairs.[209]

According to the report, the personal identities of the young administrators are systematically broken down such that in accordance with the esprit de corps of the ministry, he will loyally and obediently entirely take on his functionary role in the ministerial power pyramid.[210] It all sounds quite lethal, but according to the report, it all takes place in a 'friendly' atmosphere. This is why it is referred to as covert disciplining. Disciplining never treads forward nakedly, as it does in the disciplining of soldiers on the marching field. It is by achieving power over the case that the administrator loses power over himself and totally takes on the role, which is infused with what the report calls the 'ministry identity', which equates to Milgram's description of the agentic state.[211] The young functionary is integrated objectively into the ministry identity through the work routine known as the 'higher-lower referent system'. This system is based on the functionary preparing cases by seeing how similar earlier cases were handled. Then he asks for comments from older functionaries. These commentaries are not discussions, as by definition the more senior functionary, the 'higher referent' is always right. What occurs here is what in Milgram's experiment could be called an objective construction of the agentic state. With Milgram, this only functions as long as the authority relations are clearly demarcated. In a case where the young functionary is confronted with two department leaders with differing opinions, according to the report, it can be very difficult for the young functionary to formulate and give his proposal, because he doesn't know which of the department leaders is going to read his proposal, and therefore doesn't know which authority he should refer to. In such a situation, the young functionary has to begin to consider his own position on how the proposal should be written.

Disciplining can, according to the report, be carried out because the individual stands alone in the system, without any rights and without any group to look to for support. Disciplining is carried out objectively through a heavy work load, combined with the young functionary's aspiration to have a successful career. In this way the energies of the young functionary are bound to the ministry, while at the same time a feeling of inadequacy is built up, which breaks down the personality and fertilizes the ground for the ministerial identity. The functionary's life-world is then limited to the ministerial horizon, apart from occasional visits to his family. Finally, this disciplining process separates the functionaries who cannot be subordinated. The authors of the report cannot really promise anything to these people, even if they do their best. They talk about the employees having to form groups which can help individuals withstand the pressure from the system for conformity. But the authors must admit that this goes against the career principle itself in the ministry. Their conclusion is clear enough: It will usually cost you your career if you want to escape the agentic state.

'... Not the Real Reason, but the Best Possible One'

This description can be illustrated by the Tamil Affair. The Tamil Affair is rich in examples of obedient civil servants. One example is the delayed/evasive answer on part of Frederik Schydt, director of the Danish Immigration Service to Arne Piil Christensen, the general-secretary of the Danish Refugee Commission.[212] None of the civil servants involved in the matter were in doubt as to whether the Tamil refugees had a legal right to be united with their families in Denmark. In spite of this, Frederik Schydt sent a stalling letter to Arne Piil Christensen in which he explained that it was due to the prioritizing of resources at the Directorate that the uniting of Tamil family cases were not yet processed. What is interesting to us however, is the explanation that the office leader, Johan Reimann, gave in the investigative legal proceedings of Schydt's stalling answer:

> One could simply have said that the family unification cases were stopped because Tamils should be in Sri Lanka, but that in individual cases permission was granted because we are 'so nice'. If one did that, it would have been the same as 'shooting' the Minister, and that would have been – according to (Reimann's) opinion – a display of gross disloyalty to the Minister. One therefore had to find another reason. ... This reason was the lowering of their priority, which was given in the letter to Piil Christensen, this was ...not the real reason, but the best possible one.[213]

What is interesting here is that the image of loyalty which emerged in Milgram's experiment is entirely confirmed here.

The court of inquiry made the following comments:

> In the court of inquiry's opinion, there is no reasonable doubt, at least among the leading civil servants at the beginning of April 1988, that the foot-dragging with the cases probably was against the law, and from the middle of August 1988, clearly was illegal.
>
> In this situation, the loyalty obligations of the civil servants towards the issued order ceases, and this is replaced by an obligation to see that the unlawful situation is ended.[214]

The example shows the extent to which the agentic state can dominate a ministry. The obedient administrator is not just a theoretical construction. On the contrary, it is an entirely normal praxis which lies at the foundation of the administrator's ethical learning.

The Administrator's Ethical Education

Considerations about the ethical education of the administrator must take its point of departure in Milgram's conclusion that there are no limits to the administrator's obedience. The relevant question here is what can be done to prevent the administrator from acting out of blind obedience and encourage him to take an independent position on his actions. This question is ultimately about how the administrator can be brought out of the agentic state and act autonomously within the administration, such that he can be responsible for his own actions. However, we immediately land right back in the contradiction between the administrator as a person and as a role. The administrator does *not* define his own tasks in his role as administrator.

They are defined by his supervisors. But the administrator is personally held responsible for the actions he carries out on the order of his supervisors.

It is obvious that more than an heroic person is needed to resolve this contradiction. The problem is that the action is defined and ordered by someone other than the one who is to carry out and bear responsibility for it. The agentic state can in this way become the basic condition in administration, while at the same time, the administrator can be held responsible for his actions in the agentic state.

This contradiction, from a general perspective, cannot be resolved by referring to the individual's morality. Ulrich Horst Petersen's stoic distance can be a solution for an individual person; but it cannot be a general solution, because it would require that everyone participates in the general, ironic dissolution of the agentic state. This is not now the case, and there is little reason to believe that it will be in the future. Milgram's experiment shows this ever so clearly. The disturbing thing about Milgram's experiment is precisely that the agentic state appears to be the normal condition. Autonomy appears to be exceptional. When the *Den skjulte disciplinering* (Covert Disciplining) report recommends that groups be formed which can resist the pressure from leadership, what is proposed cannot be of general interest, because the proposal, also according to the opinion of report's authors, is based upon the members of the group being aware that this will harm their careers. But it is precisely the career which comprises the dynamic binding strap to the hierarchic order. Finally, mention is made in many places in the court of inquiry's *Beretning om Tamilsagen* (Report on the Tamil Affair) of the administrator's obligation to uphold the law and refuse to comply if orders go against the law. But the Tamil Affair is a living example that even in the cases where the law is unambiguously clear, which was the case with the Tamil family unifications, this didn't help much. There is no empirical evidence of it in general, being possible to put personal morality up against obedience. The theoretical explanation is already given above in Milgram's investigation. The blind obedience in the agentic state is not created by personal morality falling by the wayside. On the contrary, the administrator orients his *personal* morality towards loyally fulfilling the obligations which are laid upon him in his *role* as administrator. What is problematic is the form which the administrator's personal morality takes.

The administrator's personal morality in the role of administrator, according to Milgram's experiment, is formed by the authority relations present in the wider social relations within the administrative institution. If one wants to promote the administrator's own personal morality, one has to take hold of the authority relations in these social relations. Zygmunt Bauman, in his reading of Milgram's experiment, concluded that responsibility in the bureaucratic institution becomes fluid, because the one always points to another, who always has a third to point to. Bauman believes that bureaucratic organization in its entirety comes to function as a responsibility dissolving instrument.[215]

There is, however, an opening in Milgram's experiment. An interesting situation was shown that when the participant was subjected to two authorities issuing contradicting orders, the participant's obedience abated.[216] In the experiment with two authorities, the participant was simultaneously confronted with two experiment leaders, who sat next to each other. Both gave the same message up to the application of 150 Volts. At 150 Volts, disagreement arose between the two leaders. One wanted to stop the experiment because the putative student reacted with great protests. The other wanted unconditionally to continue. The result of this experiment with 20 persons was that one stopped before the disagreement, and 18 stopped exactly at the point where the disagreement first started. The authority relationship can only continue when there is accord between the authorities. Obedient action within a bureaucracy is thus decided by an authority. It requires also that authority is unambiguous. One can thus conclude that if one is confronted by multiple authorities, there is the possibility to break blind obedience. In his conclusions about the Milgram experiment, Bauman finds that pluralism is the best preventative measure against morally normal people engaging in morally abnormal actions.[217] Bauman states in this connection that the Nazis first had to do away with all remnants of political pluralism in order to set in motion their Holocaust projects. In the Soviet Union, the systematic reduction of real and supposed enemies seriously first began when the remaining social autonomy and the political pluralism reflected in it, was decimated. The individual moral conscience is best heard, according to Bauman, in the tumult of political and social disagreement.

It is, however, insufficient merely to generally confess an allegiance to political pluralism. We must recognize that Milgram's experiment was undertaken in a country with a reactively developed pluralism. It is also worth recalling that Milgram in part took inspiration for his experiment from pluralist USA's war in Vietnam. The point made in Milgram's experiment is precisely that the experiment participant and the experimental institution are separated from their pluralistic social environment and life horizon, in spite of being in the experimental environment for only the one hour set aside for the experiment. It is insufficient to appeal to pluralism in general. It is necessary that pluralism be brought into each institution. But this goes directly against the hierarchical construction of bureaucratic institutions. It appears that two irreconcilable social principles confront each other here. These two principles belong to two different forms of action rationality, namely goal-oriented rationality on the one hand and the rationality of communicative action on the other. What is meant by goal-oriented rational action, as laid out in Chapter 1, is an action characterized by the rational choice of means to attain a particular goal. What is meant by communicative action, as also outlined in Chapter 1, is communication between equal partners. One could be tempted here to untie this Gordian knot by sawing through it and proposing that the solution must be that communicative action should come to dominate. Such a claim would not lead to much in the so-called real world. Furthermore, it might not even be desirable. In a democratic society, there principally must be a hierarchic relationship between politics and bureaucracy, and this hierarchy must also apply within the bureaucratic institution. Thus, hierarchy itself is not the problem. The problem is that hierarchy drags the agentic state with it. The problem is, put concisely, how one can retain hierarchy while at the same time allowing the individual agents to retain their autonomy in the hierarchical institution.

At first glance, this appears impossible. But *in principle* it isn't so impossible, as it is possible to distinguish between role and person. It is not the person who is to act obediently in the hierarchy, it is the person in his role. But it is the person who is to bear responsibility for his actions in the bureaucracy, and the person as citizen can be brought before the legal system. This does not mean that the person in his role as administrator must find all of his actions good. The distinction between person and role allows, in a moral understanding, the person to carry out an action which he personally would not deem good. But the person must *not*, from a moral point of view, carry out in his role as administrator an action which he finds abhorrent. This means that the person should refuse to carry out actions which he cannot take responsibility for.

This understanding of the rights and duties of the individual person is generally acknowledged in modern democratic society. It is grounded in human rights and it is grounded in the basic principles of the rule of law. The problem is how this can be brought into administration in such a way that the individual administrator can take these principles into consideration when deciding how he will act. The solution must be openness in administration.

Publicity in administration has two meanings. The first is that other citizens can see into the administration; in other words, transparency. The other meaning is that the administrator himself can express himself publicly. Both meanings will be looked at here.

One must begin with the first meaning, which has to do with the opportunity for citizens to look into the administration. In this way, the administrator can be held accountable by persons other than his superiors. This accountability can represent many authorities. As mentioned, this could be an individual citizen's personal interest in administrative transparency, it could be the political institution's interest in seeing how a particular case is dealt with, it could be a competing institution's interest in keeping an eye on the institution in question, it could be the press's interest in a particular issue, it could be the legal system's interest in upholding the legal order (rule of law). What is interesting here is that these many different institutions, interests, etc. all transcend their own particularity and interests, in as much as they, as Habermas would say, must refer to the general language or communicative action.

We then arrive at the second meaning of publicity. It may be evident that the citizen who plays the role of administrator has the same right to participate in this discussion. According to the law, the administrator has full freedom of expression.[218] But he should also have the opportunity to use this right. It is in order to create this opportunity that an ethical publicity should be created in administration.[219] However, it does not help to construct a legally secured ethical public arena in the administration if the administrators are not interested in using their freedom of expression. The Danish Association of Lawyers and Economists (*DJØF*) created a commission as a result of the Tamil Affair, under the leadership of Lars Nordskov Nielsen, resulting in the publication of a report, *Fagligt etiske principper i offentlig administration* (Professional Ethical Principles in Public Administration).[220] In the report, freedom of expression is extensively dealt with. In the report, it is stated that based on hearings with civil servants, there appears to be a widespread belief among public civil servants that the freedom of expression that they are legally guaranteed is not normally used, and that in the administration there is normally an 'unwritten rule' that the employees should not speak out critically about their own work areas, and that it is usual that drafts of articles to journals, newspapers, etc., which do not belong to one's work tasks, should be shown to the nearest supervisor.[221] The Tamil Affair hearings uncovered an 'almost over-loyal position' among at least some of the public civil servants. There were even some civil servants who used the common Danish saying 'he who doesn't like the smell in the bakery...'.[222] It was laconically noted in the report that from an ethical perspective, if one wanted to encourage the participation of civil servants in the public debate, the point of departure should hardly be a documented, individual, suppressed need for expression, but rather a consideration as to whether the social value, including the democratically oriented value to which it is attached, of freedom of expression could be used to a greater extent.[223]

The result one reaches is very much dependent upon what method you use. Calling Milgram's experiments into mind, it is both obvious and frightening that it would be wrong to expect that administrators would speak out about their suppressed need for expression. This confirms my thesis that formal pluralism, as Zygmunt Bauman concludes in his analysis of Milgram's experiment, is not sufficient. On the other hand, it is not sufficient, as the DJØF report recommends, to want to 'use' the social value of freedom of expression. We stand before one of the most essential connections between democratic rule and administration. The point seems to be, if we follow Milgram, that the only way for the administrator to participate in the democratic discussion, as is desired in the DJØF report, is if transparency for the public is increased to the degree that the democratic discussion attains equal or higher authority for the individual administrator than the authority of his superiors. This is not just a matter of substituting one form of authority with another, in this case the substitution of the previous authority in the administration with that of the democratic discussion. The essential point is that there is a shift to an entirely different form of authority. It must be kept in mind that the democratic discussion points back to and involves the person (administrator) himself; to his conversing with the other. In the discussion, all relations are open to questioning; in the discussion, all authority can be dissolved. The principle of the conversation is the dissolution of all authoritative relations. In the French Revolution this came to expression by the replacement of the prince as the ultimate authority by 'the empty space of power', a nothing from which all basis for authority springs. It is this that comprises the principle of publicity.[224]

If we look beyond the heroes of morality of which, from a sociological perspective, there are few in society, one must admit that the ethical training of the administrator is directly proportional to the living discussion in a democracy. One can construct many ethical principles, but this does not help in ethically forming/educating the administrator if there is no living discussion and living democracy. The authors of the report, 'Professional Ethical Principles in Public Administration' know this. The question, according to the authors, is not whether ethical guidelines should be set.[225] Such guidelines already exist. The question is whether they should be written down. When the authors choose to equip themselves with what they call 'a draft of principles for guidance' on professional ethics in administration, it is because such guidance can lead to the 'consciousness raising', 'stating', 'clarifying', and 'concretizing' of the general morality associated with administration.[226] In this way, 'Professional Ethical Principles in Public Administration' can, together with a number of other publications, be seen not just as a sign of a crisis in democracy, but also as a contribution to the ethical education of the administrator. But this general morality will only be of interest to the ordinary administrator if these rules have real importance to him. Ultimately, this can occur by holding him responsible for his actions. There is no doubt that the Tamil Affair has been a living schooling for many administrators. The Tamil Affair, as well as a number of other scandals, has led to an increased interest in what it means to act appropriately as an administrator. It is no longer sufficient to be an obedient administrator. Ethics has become an unavoidable issue within administration in modern democratic society. This is why there is a close connection between administration, ethics and democracy.

Notes

1 Per Knudsen: 'Udlændinge-chef blev Hornslet svar skyldig', in: Dagbladet *Information*, 16.01.96, p.7. See also *Beretning om Tamilsagen*, Copenhagen 1992, p.2201 ff.

2 Carsten Henrichsen: *Tamilsagen,* Copenhagen 1993, p.46.

3 Peter Gundelach and Ole Riis: *Danskernes værdier*, Copenhagen 1992, p.178 ff.

4 Martin Basse and Oluf Jørgensen: *Åbenhed i forvaltningen*, Copenhagen 1986, p.27 ff.

5 Habermas: *Theorie des kommunikativen Handelns*, vol.II, Frankfurt am Main 1981, p.114. Habermas: *Faktizität und Geltung*, Frankfurt am Main 1992, p.394. Mikael Carleheden: 'Utopien om et demokratisk samfund', in: *Social Kritik,* n.29, Copenhagen 1993, p.83.

6 Max Weber: 'Die 'Objektivität' sozialwissenschaftlicher und sozialpolitischer Erkenntnis', in: Max Weber, *Methodologische Schriften*, Frankfurt am Main 1968.

7 See Theodor Adorno: *Negative Dialektik*, Frankfurt am Main 1980. See especially the third part, Chapter 1, 'Freiheit. Zur Metakritik der praktischen Vernunft', p.211 ff.

8 On this point see Hegel's prelude to his philosophy of law, where he discusses the problem of understanding the idea of the reasonable in the multiple forms of social reality. G.W.F. Hegel: *Grundlinien der Philosophie des Rechts*, Hamburg 1955, p.14 ff. (1821 edition, p.XX ff.)

9 Marshall Berman: *All That is Solid Melts into Air*, New York 1982.

10 Max Weber: *Gesammelte Aufsätze zur Religionsoziologie*, Tübingen 1920, vol.I, p.1.

11 Weber (1920), I, p.10-12. Habermas: *Der philosophische Diskurs der Moderne*, Frankfurt am Main 1985, p.9.

12 Weber (1920), I, p.12.

13 Habermas: *Theorie des kommunikativen Handelns*, Frankfurt am Main 1981, vol.I, p.305.

14 Weber (1920), I, p.12.

15 Ibid., p.198.

16 Ibid., p.198-199.

17 Ibid., p.202.

18 Weber (1968), p.181-182.

19 Habermas (1981), I, p.304-306, 320-321.

20 Ibid., p.321; 328.
21 Ibid., p.326-327.
22 Ibid., p.328-329.
23 Ibid., p.329.
24 Ibid., p.329-330.
25 Ibid., p.330.
26 Weber (1920), I, p.567.
27 Ibid., p.570.
28 Habermas (1981), I, p.330-331.
29 Ibid., p.331-332.
30 Ibid., p.345-346.
31 Niklas Luhmann: *Legitimation durch Verfahren*, Neuwied 1969.
32 Alf Ross: *Ret og Retfærd,* Copenhagen 1953, p.365. Emphasis added.
33 Max Weber: *Wirtschaft und Gesellschaft*, Tübingen 1976, p.124.
34 Johannes Wincklemann: *Legitimität und Legalität in Max Weber's Herrschaftssoziologie*, Tübingen 1952. Jürgen Habermas: *Legitimationsprobleme im Spätkapitalismus*, Frankfurt am Main 1973, p.133. K. Eder: 'Zur Rationalisierungsproblematik des modernen Rechts', in: *Soziale Welt*, n.2, Göttingen 1978, p.247 ff.
35 Max Weber (1968), p.210-213.
36 Ibid., p.212.
37 Ibid., p.212.
38 Ibid., p.212.
39 Habermas (1981), I, p.361.
40 Weber (1976), p.507.
41 Habermas (1981), I, p.365.
42 Ibid., p.369.
43 Weber (1968), p.4.
44 Weber (1976), p.12.
45 Weber (1968), p.26.
46 Schluchter: *Die Entwicklung des okzidentalen Rationalismus*, Tübingen 1979, p.192.
47 Habermas (1981), I, p.381.
48 Ibid., p.385.
49 Ibid., p.386.
50 Ibid., p.387.
51 Aristotle: *Politics*, London 1977, p.10 (1253a10). Øjvind Larsen: 'Det imaginære demokrati', in: *Dansk Sociologi,* n.2, vol.6, Copenhagen 1995.
52 Habermas (1981), I, p.388.
53 John L. Austin: *How to do Things with Words*, Oxford 1962, second edition 1976. J.R. Searle: *Speech Acts*, London 1969.

54 Habermas (1981), I, p.389.
55 Ibid., p.394.
56 Ibid., p.395-396.
57 Ibid., p.396.
58 Ibid., p.400.
59 Ibid., p.406.
60 Ibid., p.406.
61 Ibid., p.410.
62 Ibid., p.365.
63 Ibid., p.413.
64 Ibid., p.437-438.
65 Ibid., p.441-444.
66 Ibid., p.442-444.
67 Ibid., p.445-446.
68 Ibid., p.445.
69 Ibid., p.446-448.
70 Ibid., p.447-448.
71 Ibid., p.449.
72 Ibid., p.451.
73 Ibid., p.452.
74 Habermas (1981), II, p.206.
75 Habermas: *Philosophische-politische Profile*, Frankfurt am Main 1981, p.406 ff.
76 Habermas (1981), II, p.223.
77 Ibid., p.224.
78 Ibid., p.225-226.
79 This is based upon Ole Marquart: 'Menneskerettighedserklæringen – den idéhistoriske baggrund', in: Jens Erik Kristensen: *Menneskerettigheder,* Copenhagen 1989, p.47 ff.
80 Jan Ifversen: 'Menneskerettighederserklæringen – demokrati og ideologi', in: Jens Erik Kristensen (1989), p.22-23.
81 Ibid., p.23.
82 Ibid., p.23.
83 Claude Lefort: *Essais sur le politique, XIXe-XXe siècles*, Paris 1986, p.134. Jan Ifversen: 'Den Franske Revolution mellem demokrati og ideologi' in: *Slagmark*, n.13, Århus 1988, p.39.
84 Habermas: *Faktizität und Geltung*, Frankfurt am Main 1992. See particularly Chapter VIII, 'Zur Rolle von Zivilgesellschaft und politischer Öffentlichkeit', p.399 ff.
85 Ibid., p.134.

86 Habermas (1992), p.333 ff. See also Habermas: 'Tre normativa demokratimodeller: Om begreppet deliberativ politik', in: *Res Publica,* n.27, Stenhag 1994, p.23 ff.
87 Habermas (1994), p.30. Habermas (1992), p.33 ff.
88 Weber (1976), p.562.
89 Weber (1976), p.561-562.
90 Weber (1968), p.217. Weber (1976), p.561-562.
91 Weber (1976), p.122.
92 Ibid., p.125-126.
93 Niklas Luhmann: 'Zweck – Herrschaft – System. Grundbegriffe und Prämissen Max Webers', in: *Der Staat,* n.2, Berlin 1964.
94 Ibid., p.131.
95 Ibid., p.134.
96 Ibid., p.148.
97 Gabor Kiss: *Grundzüge und Entwicklung der Luhmannschen Systemtheorie*, Stuttgart 1986, p.80-83. Niklas Luhmann: 'Die Autopoiesis des Bewußtseins', in: *Soziale Welt*, Jahrgang 36, Heft 4, Berlin 1985, p.403.
98 Kiss (1986), p.16-17.
99 Ibid., p.86.
100 Ole Thyssen: *Penge, Magt og Kærlighed*, Copenhagen 1991, p.82 ff.
101 Ibid., p.83 ff.
102 Karl Gabriel: *Analysen der Organisationsgesellschaft*, Frankfurt am Main 1979, p.107.
103 Habermas (1981), II, p.460.
104 On this point see Torben Beck Jørgensen and Preben Melander: *Livet i offentlige organisationer*, Copenhagen 1992, p.54 ff. In this situation they speak of 'cross-pressures' (*krydspres*) on the individual administrator.
105 Öjvind Larsen: *Ethik und Demokratie*, Hamburg 1990, p.1.
106 Max Weber: 'Politik als Beruf', in: *Gesammelte politische Schriften,* Tübingen 1988, p.524.
107 Ibid., p.551-552.
108 Ibid., p.552.
109 Karl-Otto Apel: 'Konfliktlösung im Atomzeitalter als Problem einer Verantwortungsethik', in: *Diskurs und Verantwortung*, Frankfurt am Main 1990, p.250, 253.
110 Ibid., p.250.
111 Ibid., p.250.
112 Ibid., p.255.
113 Ibid., p.255-256.
114 Ibid., p.256.
115 Ibid., p.256.

116 Ibid., p.256.
117 Ibid., p.256.
118 Ibid., p.257.
119 Ibid., p.258-259.
120 Ibid., p.259-260.
121 Ibid., p.260.
122 Ibid., p.256.
123 See Øjvind Larsen: 'Den etiske problemstilling i det moderne samfund', in: *Litteratur og samfund*, n.42, Copenhagen 1987. Øjvind Larsen: *Modstandens Etik*, Copenhagen 1988.
124 Parts of the following chapter have already been published in my article 'Etik og Ytringsfrihed i Forvaltningen' in: *Retfærd*, n.57, vol.15, Copenhagen 1992.
125 Kristensen (1989), p.15.
126 See Peter Germer: *Ytringsfrihedens Væsen,* Copenhagen 1973. Martin Basse and Oluf Jørgensen: *Fortrolighed i forvaltningen,* Copenhagen 1988, p. 195 ff.
127 See Larsen (1990), p.13.
128 Jacob Hilden Winsløw: *Videnskablig Hverdag,* Copenhagen 1991, p.233.
129 Poul Andersen: 'Om Tjenstemænds Ytringsfrihed', in: Poul Andersen: *Grundtvig som rigsdagsmand og andre afhandlinger,* Copenhagen 1940. This article was later reprinted in: Poul Andersen and Carsten M. Henrichsen: *Ytringsfriheden eksisterer – men for hvem?,* Århus 1983.
130 Bent Christensen: 'Responsum vedrørende offentligt ansattes ytringsfrihed', in: *Juristen og Økonomen,* Copenhagen 1980, p.85 ff.
131 Poul Andersen: 'Om Tjenstemænds Ytringsfrihed', in: Andersen and Henrichsen (1983), p.22.
132 Ibid., p.23. See also Hanne Petersen: *Ledelse og Loyalitet,* Copenhagen 1987, p.294-296.
133 Lars Nordskov Nielsen: *Ytringsfrihed. Responsum om offentligt ansattes ytringsfrihed – med særligt sigte på overenskomstansatte DJØF'ere,* Copenhagen 1987, p.16.
134 Ole Krarup: 'Tjenestemænds ytringsfrihed', in: *Juristen,* Copenhagen 1971, p.490.
135 Nordskov Nielsen (1987), p.17. See also Torstein Eckhoff: 'Tjenstemenns lojalitetsplikt og ytringsfrihet', in: *Lov og Rett*, Oslo 1975, p.116.
136 See Nordskov Nielsen (1987), p.18-21.
137 Jørgen Dalberg-Larsen: *Loven og Livet*, Copenhagen 1987, p.184 ff. Ole Krarup: *Den juridiske virksomhed*, Copenhagen 1987, p.125.
138 Lennart Lundquist: *Byråkratisk etik,* Lund 1988, p.195-204.
139 See Øjvind Larsen: 'Etik og Modernitet', in: *Social Kritik*, n.18, Copenhagen 1992.

140 Parts of the following have been published in: 'Den lydige forvalter', *Social Kritik*, n.38, Copenhagen, 1995.
141 Zygmunt Bauman: *Modernity and the Holocaust,* Oxford 1989, p.152.
142 Ibid., p.151.
143 Ibid., p.151.
144 T.W. Adorno, *The Authoritarian Personality,* New York 1950.
145 Bauman (1989), p.153.
146 Ibid., p.153.
147 Hannah Arendt: *Eichmann in Jerusalem. A Report on the Banality of Evil*, New York 1963.
148 Ibid., p.111.
149 Ibid., p.102;103-104.
150 Ibid., p.102.
151 Ibid., p.111.
152 Ibid., p.116.
153 Ibid., p.120.
154 Ibid., p.120.
155 Ibid., p.120.
156 Ibid., p.121.
157 Ibid., p.121.
158 Immanuel Kant: *Kritik der praktischen Vernuft*, Hamburg 1974, p.177-178 (1797 edition, p.277).
159 Ibid., p.182-183 (1797 edition, p.284-285).
160 Arendt (1963), p.130.
161 This internalization of duty, according to Max Weber, must be understood in relation to Protestantism. See Øjvind Larsen, '... indtil det sidste ton fossile brændstof er gennemglødet', in: Max Weber: *Den protestantiske etik og kapitalismens ånd*, Copenhagen 1995.
162 Max Weber (1988), p.524.
163 Arendt (1963), p.130.
164 Ibid., p.130.
165 Ibid., p.134.
166 Stanley Milgram: *Obedience to Authority*, New York 1974, p.XI-XIII.
167 Ibid., p.XI-XIII.
168 Ibid., p.XI.
169 Ibid., p.133.
170 Ibid., p.34-35.
171 Ibid., p.27-28.
172 Ibid., p.32.
173 Ibid., p.121-122.
174 Ibid., p.121-122.

175 Ibid., p.121-122.
176 Ibid., p.135.
177 Ibid., p.135-144.
178 Ibid., p.138.
179 Ibid., p.143.
180 Ibid., p.145-146.
181 Ibid., p.145-146.
182 Bauman (1989), p.160-161.
183 Ibid., p.160.
184 See Benny Lihme: 'Staten som serial killer', in: *Social Kritik*, n.33, Copenhagen 1994.
185 Milgram (1974), p.75-76.
186 Ibid., p.146.
187 Ibid., p.147-148.
188 Ibid., p.147-148.
189 Ibid., p.149-150.
190 Bauman (1989), p.157-159.
191 Milgram (1974), p.153-157.
192 Ibid., p.155-156.
193 Ibid., p.157-161.
194 Ibid., p.160.
195 Ibid., p.162.
196 Ibid., p. 162-164.
197 Ibid., p.186.
198 Bauman (1989), p.161-163.
199 Milgram (1974), p.186-189.
200 Ulrich Horst Petersen: 'På Slotsholmen', in: Ulrich Horst Petersen: *I mellemtiden*, Copenhagen 1986, p.76.
201 Ibid., p.82.
202 Ibid., p.85.
203 Ibid., p.89.
204 Ibid., p.89-90.
205 Ibid., p.91.
206 Ibid., p.100.
207 See Villy Sørensen's interpretation of Seneca, in: *Seneca: Humanisten ved Neros hof* (Seneca: The Humanist in the Court of Nero), Copenhagen 1976.
208 'Den skjulte disciplinering', in: *Stud. Samf.*, n.1, 1981.
209 It also builds upon Thomas Mathiesen: *Den skjulte disciplinering*, Oslo 1978.
210 'Den skjulte disciplinering', p.4.
211 Ibid., p.5.
212 *Beretning om Tamilsagen* (1992), p.2123-2124.

213 Ibid., p.2124.
214 Ibid., p.2199.
215 Bauman (1989), p.161-163.
216 Milgram (1974), p.105-107.
217 Bauman (1989), p.165-166.
218 Øjvind Larsen: 'Etik og Ytringsfrihed i Forvaltningen', in: *Retfærd,* n.57, Copenhagen 1992.
219 Øjvind Larsen: 'Etik og Forvaltning', in: *Social Kritik,* n.18, Copenhagen 1992.
220 *Fagligt etiske principper i offentlig administration*, A report given by DJØF's professional ethics workgroup, Copenhagen 1993.
221 Ibid., p.173.
222 Ibid., p.179.
223 Ibid., p.179.
224 See Øjvind Larsen: 'Det imaginære demokrati', in: *Dansk Sociologi,* n.2, vol.6, Copenhagen 1995.
225 *Fagligt etiske principper i offentlige administration* (1993), p.191.
226 Ibid., p.193, 233 ff.

Bibliography

Adorno, Theodor W., *The Authoritarian Personality*, New York 1950.

Adorno, Theodor, *Negative Dialektik*, Frankfurt am Main 1980.

Andersen, Poul, 'Om Tjenestemænds Ytringsfrihed', in: Poul Andersen, *Grundtvig som rigsdagsmand og andre afhandlinger*, Copenhagen 1940.

Andersen, Poul, 'Om Tjenestemænds Ytringsfrihed', in: Poul Andersen og Carsten M. Henrichsen, *Ytringsfriheden eksisterer – men for hvem?*, Århus 1983.

Apel, Karl-Otto, 'Konfliktlösung im Atomzeitalter als Problem einer Verantwortungsethik', in: *Diskurs und Verantwortung*, Frankfurt am Main 1988.

Arendt, Hannah, *Eichmann in Jerusalem. A Report on the Banality of Evil*, New York 1963.

Aristoteles, *Politics*, The Loeb Classical Library, vol XXI, London 1977.

Austin, J.L., *How to do Things with Words*, Oxford 1962; 2. edition1976.

Basse, Martin, og Oluf Jørgensen, *Åbenhed i forvaltningen*, Copenhagen 1986.

Basse, Martin, og Oluf Jørgensen, *Fortrolighed i forvaltningen*, Copenhagen 1988.

Bauman, Zygmunt, *Modernity and the Holocaust*, Cambridge 1989.

Beck Jørgensen, Torben, og Preben Melander, *Livet i offentlige organisationer*, Copenhagen 1992.

Beretning om Tamilsagen, Copenhagen 1992.

Bogason, Peter, *Organisation og Beslutning*, Copenhagen 1988.

Carleheden, Mikael, 'Utopien om et demokratisk samfund', in: *Social Kritik,* n.29, Copenhagen 1993.

Christensen, Bent, 'Responsum vedrørende offentligt ansattes ytringsfrihed', in: *Juristen og Økonomen*, Copenhagen 1980.

Dalberg-Larsen, Jørgen, *Lovene og Livet*, Copenhagen 1991.

'Den skjulte disciplinering', in: *Stud. Samf.*, n.1, 1981.

Eckhoff, Torstein, 'Tjenestemenns lojalitetsplikt og ytringsfrihet', in: *Lov og Rett*, Oslo 1975.

Eder, K., 'Zur Rationalisierungsproblematik des modernen Rechts', in: *Soziale Welt*, n.2, Göttingen 1978.

Fagligt etiske principper i offentlig administration, Betænkning afgivet af DJØF's fagligt etiske arbejdsgruppe, Copenhagen 1993.

Forester, John, *Planning in the Face of Power*, Berkeley and Los Angeles 1989.

Gabriel, Karl, *Analysen der Organisationsgesellschaft*, Frankfurt am Main 1979.

Germer, Peter, *Ytringsfrihedens Væsen*, Copenhagen 1973.

Gundelach, Peter, og Ole Riis, *Danskernes værdier*, Copenhagen 1992.
Habermas, Jürgen, *Borgerlig Offentlighed*, Copenhagen 1971.
Habermas, Jürgen, *Legitimationsprobleme im Spätkapitalismus*, Frankfurt am Main 1973.
Habermas, Jürgen, *Philosophische-politische Profile*, Frankfurt am Main 1981.
Habermas, Jürgen, *Theorie des kommunikativen Handelns*, vol.I-II, Frankfurt 1981.
Habermas, Jürgen, *Der philosophische Diskurs der Moderne*, Frankfurt am Main 1985.
Habermas, Jürgen, *Faktizität und Geltung*, Frankfurt am Main 1992.
Habermas, Jürgen, 'Tre normativa demokratimodeller: Om begreppet deliberativ politik', in: *Res Publica*, n.27, Stehag 1994.
Hegel, G. W. F., *Grundlinien der Philosophie des Rechts*, Hamburg 1955.
Henrichsen, Carsten, 'Offentligt ansattes ytringsfrihed i forvaltningsteoretisk belysning', in: *Juristen og Økonomen*, Copenhagen 1981.
Henrichsen, Carsten, *Tamilsagen*, Copenhagen 1993.
Hilden Winsløw, Jakob, *Videnskabelig Hverdag*, Copenhagen 1991.
Horst Petersen, Ulrich, 'På Slotsholmen', in: Ulrich Horst Petersen, *I mellemtiden*, Copenhagen 1986.
Ifversen, Jan, 'Den Franske Revolution mellem demokrati og ideologi', in: *Slagmark*, n.13, Århus 1988.
Ifversen, Jan, 'Menneskerettighedserklæringen – demokrati og ideologi', in: Jens Erik Christensen, *Menneskerettigheder*, Copenhagen 1989.
Jepsen, Jørgen, 'Etik og Styring', in: Ellen-Margrethe Basse og Vibeke Jensen: *Regulering og Styring*, vol.II, Copenhagen 1990.
Kant, Immanuel, *Kritik der praktischen Vernunft*, udgivet af Karl Vorländer, Hamburg 1974.
Kiss, Gabor, *Grundzüge und Entwicklung der Luhmannschen Systemtheorie*, Stuttgart 1986.
Knudsen, Per: 'Udlændinge-chef blev Hornslet svar skyldig', in: Dagbladet *Information*, d. 16.01.92.
Krarup, Ole, 'Tjenestemænds ytringsfrihed', in: *Juristen*, Copenhagen 1971.
Krarup, Ole, *Den juridiske virksomhed*, Copenhagen 1987.
Kristensen, Jens Erik, *Menneskerettigheder*, Copenhagen 1989.
Larsen, Øjvind, *Den etiske tænkemådes tilblivelse i den demokratiske bystat Athen*, Roskilde 1986.
Larsen, Øjvind, 'Den etiske problemstilling i det moderne samfund', in: *Litteratur og Samfund*, n.42, Copenhagen 1987.
Larsen, Øjvind, *Modstandens Etik*, Copenhagen 1988.
Larsen, Öjvind, *Ethik und Demokratie,* Hamburg 1990.
Larsen, Øjvind, 'Etik og Forvaltning', in: *Social Kritik,* n.18, Copenhagen 1992.

Larsen, Øjvind, 'Etik og Modernitet', in: *Social Kritik,* n.18, Copenhagen 1992.

Larsen, Øjvind, 'Etik og Ytringsfrihed i Forvaltningen', in: *Retfærd,* n.57, vol.15., Copenhagen 1992.

Larsen, Øjvind, 'Den lydige forvalter', in: *Social Kritik,* n.38, Copenhagen 1995.

Larsen, Øjvind, 'Det imaginære demokrati', in: *Dansk Sociologi,* n.2, vol.6., Copenhagen 1995.

Larsen, Øjvind, '... indtil det sidste ton fossile brændstof er gennemglødet', in: Max Weber, *Den protestantiske etik og kapitalismens ånd*, Copenhagen 1995.

Lefort, Claude, *Essais sur le politique, XIXe-XXe siècles*, Paris 1986.

Lihme, Benny, 'Staten som serial killer', in: *Social Kritik,* n.33, Copenhagen 1994.

Luhmann, Niklas, 'Zweck – Herrschaft – System. Grundbegriffe und Prämissen Max Webers', in: *Der Staat*, n.2, Berlin 1964.

Luhmann, Niklas, *Legitimation durch Verfahren*, Neuwied 1969.

Luhmann, Niklas, 'Die Autopoiesis des Bewußtseins', in: *Soziale Welt*, Jahrgang 36, Heft 4, Berlin 1985.

Lundquist, Lennart, *Byråkratisk Etik*, Lund 1988.

Løgstrup, K.E., 'Den offentlige forvaltning og magtstrukturen i samfundet', in: *Nordisk Administrativt Tidsskrift*, n.60, Copenhagen 1979.

Marquart, Ole, 'Menneskerettighedserklæringen – den idéhistoriske baggrund', in: Jens Erik Kristensen, *Menneskerettigheder*, Copenhagen 1989.

Mathiesen, Thomas, *Den skjulte disciplinering*, Oslo 1978.

Milgram, Stanley, *Obedience to Authority*, New York 1974.

Nordskov Nielsen, Lars, *Ytringsfrihed. Responsum om offentligt ansattes ytringsfrihed – med særligt sigte på overenskomstansatte DJØF'ere*, Copenhagen 1987.

Petersen, Hanne, *Ledelse og Loyalitet*, Copenhagen 1987.

Rohr, John A., 'Ethics in Public Administration: A State-of-the-Discipline Report', in: Naomi B. Lynn og Aaron Wildavsky, *Public Administration. The State of the Discipline*, Chatham, New Jersey 1990.

Ross, Alf, *Ret og Retfærdighed*, Copenhagen 1953.

Schluchter, Wolfgang, *Die Entwicklung des okzidentalen Rationalismus*, Tübingen 1979.

Searle, J.R., *Speech Acts*, London 1969.

Sørensen, Villy, *Seneca: Humanisten ved Neros hof*, Copenhagen 1976.

Thyssen, Ole, *Penge, Magt og Kærlighed*, Copenhagen 1991.

Weber, Max, *Gesammelte Aufsätze zur Religionssoziologie*, vol.I, Tübingen 1920.

Weber, Max, 'Politik als Beruf', in: *Gesammelte Politische Schriften*, Tübingen 1988.

Weber, Max, *Methodologische Schriften*, Frankfurt am Main 1968.

Weber, Max, *Den protestantiske etik og kapitalismens ånd*, Copenhagen 1995.

Weber, Max, *Wirtschaft und Gesellschaft*, Tübingen 1976.
Winckelmann, Johannes, *Legitimität und Legalität in Max Webers Herrschaftssoziologie*, Tübingen 1952.
Winsløw, Jakob Hilden, *Videnskabelig Hverdag*, Copenhagen 1991.